Isn't Her Grace Amazing!

American gospel singer Clara
Ward (1924–1973) performing
live onstage circa 1965.

Isn't Her Grace Amazing!

THE WOMEN WHO CHANGED GOSPEL MUSIC

Cheryl Wills

AMISTAD
— 35 —

An Imprint of HarperCollins*Publishers*

FIRST EDITION

Designed by Sandy Lawrence; adapted by Terry McGrath/Ad Librum

Library of Congress Cataloging-in-Publication Data is available upon request.

ISBN 978-0-06-305098-3

22 23 24 25 26 WOR 10 9 8 7 6 5 4 3 2 1

Pastor Shirley Caesar performing during the Thirty-Fifth Anniversary Celebration for Bishop Thomas Dexter "T. D." Jakes Sr. at the AT&T Performing Arts Center on June 8, 2012, in Dallas, Texas.

Singer Tamela Mann performs onstage during
the 2013 BET Awards at Nokia Theatre LA Live
on June 30, 2013, in Los Angeles, California.

To my Holy Ghost–filled, fire-baptized, choir-directing,
and piano-playing grandmother,
Sister Opal Wills (1927–2019)

Psalm 100

1 Make a joyful noise unto the Lord, all ye lands.

2 Serve the Lord with gladness: come before his presence with singing.

3 Know ye that the Lord he is God: it is he that hath made us, and not we ourselves; we are his people, and the sheep of his pasture.

4 Enter into his gates with thanksgiving, and into his courts with praise: be thankful unto him, and bless his name.

5 For the Lord is good; his mercy is everlasting; and his truth endureth to all generations.

Yolanda Adams performs onstage
during Peace Starts with Me concert
at Nassau Coliseum on November 12,
2018, in Uniondale, New York.

CONTENTS

Aretha Franklin,
live in Palermo.

Introduction

From the moment I entered the world, gospel music was my everything! My grandmother Opal was a pianist and choir director. My grandfather Fred was the guitarist and pastor. My dad, Clarence, also a guitarist, was the deacon. I was baptized into the very sounds that make this historical book so personal for me.

As soon as I could sit up straight and hold my own weight, I kept time to their Tennessee-inspired rhythms with my trusty tambourine. Our little storefront church was in Queens, New York, but the traditions in our sanctuary sprang from the Deep South. My family brought the Mississippi Delta sounds with them when they migrated from Haywood County to New York City. The whole family worked up a sweat every Sunday morning as they sang what they routinely called "the songs of Zion." Songs made famous by many of the recording artists featured in this book. Songs that soothed the soul for Black folks even as chaos erupted on the gritty streets and in the countrysides of America.

To hear my grandmother's alto voice bounce off the walls and sweep like Holy Ghost fire across a congregation of just a few dozen Black folks was a sight to see. Sister Wills, as they called my grandma, could really *really* sing. Just like Inez Andrews or Dorothy Norwood, gospel stars whom my grandmother absolutely adored, she would start out softly with her eyes closed as her short stubby fingers played the classic gospel chord of F-sharp. And after a few rounds of the same chorus, her voice would rise and grow stronger, and it was impossible for the church members to remain in their seats. Lucky for me, I had a front-row seat to this weekly Christian drama. I squeezed next to my grandmother on a black piano stool, astounded by the grip she had on the audience as they screamed and shouted her name: "SING, SISTER WILLS, SING!" And sometimes when the music reached its feverish pitch, singing gave way to shouting. It was a head-scratcher for little ole me, as I struggled to understand what provoked men and women to dance in the spirit and scream "Hallelujah!" and "Thank you, Jesus!" I always kept my eye on Grandma, as she sometimes strayed from her black piano and left me there alone . . . with only the sounds of my dad's and grandpa's electric guitars and foot-stomping and hand-clapping that nearly raised the roof of this dusty church.

Before I entered kindergarten, our Sunday morning rituals taught me about the power of gospel music, and it was unlike anything I saw on *Sesame Street*. As a youngster, I sometimes wondered, is this just our family or do other people "praise the Lord" like this?

It wasn't until my grandmother cranked up her old record player, which was in a huge furniture-like console in the early 1970s, and gently put the needle on a well-worn black disc that I realized there were lots of ladies who sang just like Sister Wills. "Stone Singers" like Albertina Walker, whose Savoy label logo is still burned into my memory. On Saturday afternoons, when Grandma put a metal hot comb on a big white stove to press my hair for the next day, I'll never forget how Grandma hummed along to Walker, Inez Andrews, Shirley Caesar, and other members of the Caravans as they belted out "Oh Mary, don't you weep." I can still see their album cover with the four women standing shoulder to shoulder in black choir robes with pink collars, and there was one man in a tan suit with a bow tie. With the smell of burned hair hanging in the air, I studied the album covers front and back, my grandmother whispering, "Sing, Inez, sing!" as she straightened the left side of my curly hair and then the right side. It was only

later that I realized this classic recording was made in 1958, about eight years before I was born, but Grandma wore that record out like it was brand-new.

Grandma also secretly rooted for the women gospel singers in the mid-twentieth century, and it was my great honor to immortalize them in this book. The Davis Sisters, Mahalia Jackson, Marion Williams, Sister Rosetta Tharpe, who fascinated me because she played the guitar just like my grandpa in church, only with a lot more flash! Turns out, Grandma rooted for the women because gospel music was a man's game.

Don't get me wrong. When we had time to kill, we also listened to male gospel groups like the Soul Stirrers, the Dixie Hummingbirds, and the Pilgrim Jubilees, but it was something about when the "sisters" grabbed the microphone that changed the air in the room!

As she parted my newly straightened hair in quarters and styled a bang on my forehead, I asked my grandma why she didn't make a record like Clara Ward or Dorothy Love Coates. Grandma always brushed it off. She had a husband and two sons, and she could never imagine leaving them for a life on the road. It wasn't until I became a working adult that I fully appreciated the tremendous sacrifices every single one of these women in *Isn't Her Grace Amazing!* made to get to the top of the gospel charts. Through my research, I also learned that they faced criticism sometimes for being too "worldly" with their makeup and jewelry. My grandma prided herself as being a "holy" woman. Once she was baptized and "saved," Grandma stopped wearing makeup and earrings, and her dresses had to be well below her knee and her sleeves below her elbow. As a saved woman and mother, she had been trained to put her husband first in all things. But, in truth, Grandma was a leader, and she used her talent as a singer to make her presence known. More than a few of the singers in this book pushed back against taking a back seat and defiantly followed their hearts. Grandma admired their courage, and believe me, it took courage, as a woman, to become a gospel star! That's why this book is a dream come true for me. These gospel divas are the original "Black Girl Magic" with a Bible!

Grandma's voice was forever silenced in 2019, and like many of the singers featured in *Isn't Her Grace Amazing!*, I am resurrecting her vibrant spirit through the remarkable careers of these legendary singers who truly "made a way out of no way."

And it's because of my deep love for women in gospel music that I was hired to host one of the biggest gospel events in the country that focused on gospel women: the Essence Empowerment Festival. Although Grandma was too sick to travel with me from New York to New Orleans, I was excited to tell her how I met Grammy Award–winning artists like Yolanda Adams, whom I had the opportunity to chat with backstage before introducing her to a crowd of thousands during Independence Day weekend. Her style and long list of notable achievements include performing multiple times at the White House for different administrations, earning her a spot on this exclusive list.

I also had the honor of meeting Dottie Peoples, Kim Burrell, CeCe Winans, Tramaine Hawkins, and Mary Mary; I saw firsthand how each of these dynamic performers made tremendous personal sacrifices as they picked up the baton from the Davis Sisters, Ward, and Tharpe. It was clear to me that they loved the Lord and sang his praises, and they made no apologies for who they were and from whence they came.

Backstage, I was most struck by their impeccable sense of style! I tell ya, these ladies sparkled like diamonds from head to toe. Many times, I had to pinch myself as I peeked from behind the curtain and watched thousands scream "Hallelujah" and shout just as they did in my grandparents' little storefront church a generation ago.

As an Emmy Award–winning journalist, I experienced a special thrill interviewing Dionne Warwick for this project. She was eager to share firsthand memories of the Drinkard Singers, a pioneering group that consisted of her aunt, Cissy Houston (Whitney Houston's mom), and was managed by her mother, Mancel. The Drinkard Singers have faded into history, but Dionne was excited to know that her family was getting their just due as a powerful force in gospel music during its early years. I could see in Dionne's eyes during our virtual interview (due to the pandemic) how important her family's legacy was to her.

It is a deep honor to shine a spotlight on the legacy of these extraordinary women who elevated gospel music, each in her own way. They didn't just sing a song; they left an indelible mark. Sort of like my Sister Wills did with me and anyone who had the privilege of hearing her during her prime. Go to the Acknowledgments to find out how you can hear Sister Wills sing for yourself. My grandmother's songs still vibrate through my entire being. I remember that in her final years, she was bound to a wheelchair and dementia had set in, but her booming alto voice was the last to go. That's when I knew it was over. But Sister Wills and all the powerhouse singers who have joined her in that heavenly choir are singing and shouting about how they have overcome! And those who are still gracing the stage are pressing on.

Amen and Hallelujah!

1

QUEEN
MOTHERS

Mahalia Jackson

Born: October 26, 1911
Died: January 27, 1972
Hometown: New Orleans, Louisiana
Notable Gospel Hits: "Move On Up a Little Higher,"
"Trouble of This World," "How I Got Over"
Notable Crossover Hits: "Take My Hand, Precious Lord,"
"He's Got the Whole World in His Hands"
Awards and Accolades: Three Grammy Awards,
Grammy Lifetime Achievement Award (1973),
Gospel Music Hall of Fame (1978), Rock and
Roll Hall of Fame (1997)

Mahalia Jackson, one of the
most influential female vocalists
of the twentieth century.

Mahalia Jackson in the dressing room of Bunkyo Kokaido Hall on April 11, 1971, in Tokyo, Japan.

When Mahalia Jackson sang the stirring hymn "Trouble of the World" during the climax of the classic film *Imitation of Life*, the world was introduced to the queen of gospel, who laid the blueprint for generations of gospel singers for the next fifty years.

Mahalia, the granddaughter of slaves, began singing in churches throughout her native New Orleans as a child. She quickly became known as the "little girl with the big voice." While she was surrounded and influenced by the musical gumbo of the Crescent City, particularly the blues and jazz, Mahalia was strongly encouraged to only use her voice to sing God's praises. She was repeatedly offered more money to sing the blues, but she refused to sing in nightclubs.

By the age of sixteen, Mahalia moved to Chicago and worked as a washerwoman by day and began singing with her aunt Hannah's church choir at the Greater Salem Baptist Church. In 1934, she recorded her first song, "God's Gonna Separate the Wheat from the Tares," for just twenty-five dollars. In the late 1930s and 1940s she began touring with the father of gospel music, Thomas Dorsey. In 1946, she recorded her first million-selling single, "Move On Up a Little Higher."

In 1950, Mahalia became the first woman gospel singer to perform at Carnegie Hall in New York City, and she sang at the Newport Jazz Festival in 1956. During the mid- to late 1950s, Mahalia performed all over the globe with tours throughout Europe and Asia and was crowned the queen of gospel. She earned her first two Grammys in 1961 and 1962 for the classic gospel albums *Great Songs of Love and Faith* and *Every Time I Feel the Spirit*.

When she appeared at the world-famous Apollo Theater in 1963, Billy Mitchell, who would later become known as "Mr. Apollo," was in the audience during the spirit-filled performance, with his grandmother. "I couldn't believe the sound that was coming out of her mouth," Mitchell shared. "All you saw around the room was crying, shouting, and a waving of hands."

Jackson sings on bended knee with her arms outstretched at the Newport Jazz Festival, Newport, Rhode Island, July 7, 1957.

Jackson sings at the March on Washington for Freedom and Jobs on the steps of the Lincoln Memorial, Washington, DC, August 28, 1963. Sitting at lower right is civil rights leader Martin Luther King Jr. (1929–1968) and his wife, Coretta Scott King; between them is activist Whitney Young (1921–1971).

Even though Mahalia had a limited education, she became a consummate businesswoman and millionaire during her lifetime. Her obsession with immaculately pressing and styling her hair led to her eventually opening her own shop called Mahalia's Beauty Salon. Her fans could see her crowning glory whipping across her head as she was moved by the spirit. Mahalia was also a good cook. Her specialties were big pans of cornbread and potato salad. Mahalia called cooking "her joy." She would feed the hungry even when she didn't have much money herself. "You can't beat God giving!" Mahalia told an interviewer in 1971.

Mahalia became a prominent voice of the civil rights movement. She was also a frequently requested soloist and friend to Dr. Martin Luther King Jr. Mahalia sang "How I Got Over" and "I've Been Buked" during the historic March on Washington on August 28, 1963. She can even be heard in the background encouraging Dr. King by shouting, "Tell 'em about the dream, Martin!" Mahalia was also one of the featured soloists during Dr. King's homegoing service in April 1968.

When both Mahalia Jackson and another music great, Louis Armstrong, were at the end of their lives, one of their final collaborations was at the Newport Jazz Festival in 1970. A giant in the jazz world, Armstrong had become frail and needed to be helped onstage, while Mahalia appeared strong and lifted her gown during her "holy dance" on the outdoor stage.

"I wanna sing this song because he happened to be from my hometown," Mahalia noted as she casually fussed with her nails. She dedicated "Just a Closer Walk with Thee" to Satchmo, and Mahalia's rendition was so powerful that Louis signaled for the queen of gospel to return to the stage for an encore. The two larger-than-life figures from the Crescent City held each other in a warm embrace, and they sang together backed up by a brass band.

It was a nostalgic farewell. Armstrong transitioned exactly one year later, and about six months after that Mahalia's rich voice was also silenced forever. Her reign as the queen of gospel came to an end upon her death in 1972. Throughout her career, Mahalia reached unprecedented heights in the recording industry, with eight gospel hits, including "I Believe" and "He's Got the Whole World In His Hands," that sold more than one million copies. And her influence continues to inspire generations of women gospel singers to "move on up a little higher"!

Mahalia Jackson singing at the Lincoln Memorial during "Prayer Pilgrimage for Freedom" in Washington, DC, in 1957.

Sallie Martin

Born: November 20, 1896
Died: June 18, 1988
Hometown: Pittsville, Georgia
Notable Gospel Hits: "He's So Wonderful," "Just a Closer Walk with Thee," "God Put a Rainbow in the Clouds," "He'll Wash You Whiter Than Snow"
Awards and Accolades: Known as the queen or mother of gospel, formed the first professional female gospel group on record, cofounded National Convention of Gospel Choirs and Choruses, became a successful businesswoman and established what would become the oldest continuously operating Black gospel music publisher in the US, inducted into the Gospel Music Hall of Fame in 1991.

Sallie Martin in the 1982 documentary musical *Say Amen, Somebody*, directed by George T. Nierenberg.

If you close your eyes while listening to the great Sallie Martin, the tone and timbre of her voice could easily belong to both the blues and gospel. When you listen to her singing "He's So Wonderful" with the Refreshing Spring COGIC Children's Choir in one of her few televised performances, her voice shrills, thrills, and crescendos in all the right places. Fortunately for those singers and musicians who would eventually benefit from Sallie's incredible contributions to gospel music, Martin devoted her life to singing about her Savior and became one of the first women to pioneer this dynamic music throughout the world. In a 1985 interview, she talked about the difference between the blues and gospel: "In the blues you are singing because you are down and out, because your man or woman left you and you got real blue—or so they tell me. In gospel, you are singing about the Lord. I don't sing; the Lord just uses my tone. I don't get blue because I got the Lord in me."

Along with Willie Mae Ford Smith, Sallie was also instrumental in developing the initial sound of gospel music with Thomas Dorsey. Born and raised in Pittsville, Georgia, Sallie became an orphan after her father left the family before her birth and her mother's death in her early teens. She left her hometown because she didn't want to become a cotton picker or a domestic worker. Sallie moved to Atlanta and took on a series of jobs to support herself. She joined the Fire Baptized Holiness Church because she loved the spirit and spontaneity of the services.

Sallie had the good fortune to meet Dorsey during a choir audition in 1929. He was initially unimpressed with the dark rough quality of her voice, but he eventually invited her to join the Dorsey Trio and introduce his compositions to churches throughout the South. Sallie made her debut with the group at the Ebenezer Baptist Church. She toured with Dorsey and his groups throughout the country for nine years. Along with Willie Mae Ford Smith, she helped organize the National Convention of Gospel Choirs and Choruses (NCGCC). She served as vice president of the NCGCC until her death. In the 1940s, she branched out and formed her own group, the Sallie Martin Singers, which included her daughter Cora Martin, quartet legend Brother Joe, and the future jazz impresario Dinah Washington, who was then known as Ruth Jones.

Sallie's influence on gospel music extended far beyond the pulpit and the concert halls, as she joined forces with Dorsey to publish his compositions and increase the sale of his music. Her brilliant business sense resulted in the great popularity of his music and greater fortunes for both of them. After a dispute with Dorsey in 1940, Sallie formed her own music publishing company called Martin and Morris Music Company, which was devoted exclusively to publishing gospel sheet music.

Sallie's company published songs by some of the pioneers of gospel, including Dorothy Love Coates, James Cleveland, Lucy Campbell, and Sam Cooke. The company was the oldest Black-owned gospel music publisher in the country until its closing in 1993. Martin's pioneering business sense afforded her great wealth, and she became one of the richest women in gospel music.

Throughout her life she was a vocal proponent of the power of gospel music and bringing it to churches throughout the country. In a 1981 interview, Martin commented, "I think gospel music is a thing of the soul. People sing it if they're burdened; then again, if they feel happy, they can give it out like that. . . . People will get a message that there must be something behind this."

Inez Andrews

Born: April 14, 1929
Died: December 19, 2012
Hometown: Birmingham, Alabama
Notable Gospel Hits: "Lord, Don't Move That Mountain,"
"God's Humble Servant"
Awards and Accolades: Gospel Music Hall of Fame
(2002)

Inez Andrews,
circa 1970.

With a soaring multi-octave range that could go from contralto to first soprano, listening to the divine voice of Inez Andrews could lift you from the valley to the mountaintop. With her slender frame and elegant presence, Andrews would often surprise audiences with her powerful delivery and the classic vocals that made her one of the pioneering voices of gospel music.

"I would describe Inez Andrews as the Millie Jackson of gospel," said Tim Dillinger, gospel historian and independent researcher. "Especially in her later years, she was known for her more contemporary approach to her music and connecting with her audience with sermons and testimonies."

Andrews did not have an easy road to becoming a gospel singer. Born in Birmingham, Alabama, she followed the path of many women in her family and became a wife and mother of seven children. As a domestic worker, she often toiled for ten to twelve hours a day. After years of spinning in that hopeless cycle, she said in an interview with *Ebony* magazine, "I had an epiphany. One day, I was cooking some rice and brown beets, and I said, 'This wasn't what I wanted to do with my life. This wasn't what I wanted to be.' I felt there was something else, something better. And I said to myself, 'Is this all God planned for me?' And as I began to say that, I got a pencil and brown paper bag, and I wrote."

That epiphany led to Andrews writing a series of songs and her voice catching the ear of local gospel groups who were mesmerized by her impressive vocal range. Inez soon took on the nickname "Songbird," as she brought color and life to any arrangement that she sang. She began singing with two groups, the Carter's Choral Ensemble and the Original Gospel Harmonettes. When the Harmonettes became popular in churches throughout the 1950s, Inez became the understudy for the Harmonettes lead singer and gospel legend Dorothy Love Coates.

Coates eventually recommended that Inez audition for the classic lineup of the Caravans in the 1960s that included Shirley Caesar, Dorothy Norwood, and Albertina Walker. Inez moved to Chicago to be closer to the group, and her gospel career took off. Her soaring vocals could be heard on the group's classic recordings, including "Lord Keep Me Day by Day," "I'm Not Tired Yet," and her soul-stirring solo for "Mary, Don't You Weep." Walker, founder of the legendary Caravans, often said, "Nothing ever worked for the Caravans until Inez started whistling—hitting the high notes." This legendary lineup of the Caravans included many years of touring on the road and producing several gold albums. Andrews's version of "Mary, Don't You Weep" was covered by Aretha Franklin on her legendary gospel album *Amazing Grace*.

By 1962, Inez branched out from the Caravans, forming her own group, Inez Andrews and the Andrewettes. While Inez and the Andrewettes achieved notable acclaim, Inez was not fond of being a group leader. By the early 1970s, she went solo and scored a huge hit in 1972 with "Lord, Don't Move That Mountain." Her other hits throughout the years have included "Just for Me," "A Sinner's Prayer," and "I Appreciate."

In 2006, Inez reunited with the Caravans and recorded a reunion album that became a gold-selling album and put the quartet back on the map and at the top of the gospel charts. At the end of her storied life, she said in an interview with the *Chicago Tribune*, "I'd like to be remembered as a person who lived the life they sang about. And I would hope that my conduct in life would be such that someone would want to see me again on the other side."

Albertina Walker

Born: August 29, 1929
Died: October 8, 2010
Hometown: Chicago, Illinois
Notable Gospel Hits: "Please Be Patient with Me,"
"I Can Go to God in Prayer"
Awards and Accolades: One Grammy Award, three
Stellar Awards, three Dove Awards, National Heritage
Fellowship (2005)

Albertina Walker on
March 3, 2003, in
Dallas, Texas.

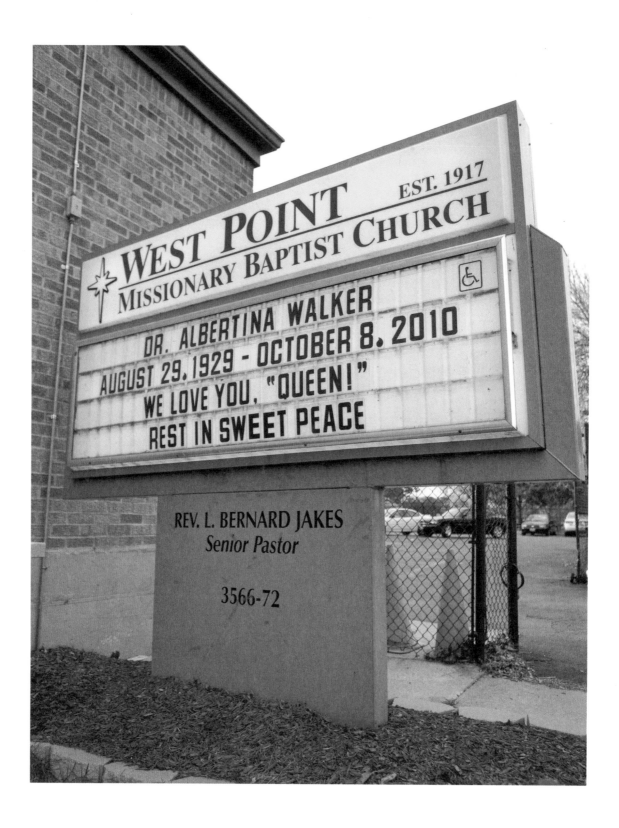

As male gospel groups were touring and making their way throughout the nation, there was a quiet revolution happening in Chicago under the brilliant genius of Albertina Walker. In 1952, Albertina and several of her sisters in song met at a recording session for a local gospel legend. When he didn't show up, Albertina and Inez Andrews took over the lead vocals for the recording, cut a local hit, and thus the legendary Caravans were born. Talk about sisters doing it for themselves!

For nearly two decades, Albertina led this powerhouse group of singers that included in its dynamic lineup Shirley Caesar, Dorothy Norwood, James Cleveland, Inez Andrews, and Dolores Washington, all of whom would become gospel legends in their own right.

Before she became a gospel sensation, Albertina began singing at just four years old in the children's choir of the West Point Baptist Church on Chicago's South Side. She had a bold personality, and she sang in nightclubs throughout Chicago during her teenage years before she committed herself to singing the Gospel. By the time Albertina was ten years old, her mother had died. While her mother's death left an early void in her life, it was as if this loss expanded Albertina's heart to become a mother figure and mentor to many gospel artists throughout her career.

One of Albertina's idols growing up was the great Mahalia Jackson. Albertina was so determined to meet Mahalia that she showed up on Mahalia's doorstep unannounced. According to Jackson's biographer Laurraine Goreau, Jackson yelled at the young budding singer, "Girl, you got so much nerves, and you even come up to my house, and I ain't even invited you and you just refuse to leave! But I can afford you because you remind me so much of myself when I was coming up."

Albertina was eventually mentored and influenced by Jackson, and she noted that Mahalia would often say to her, "Girl, you need to go sing by yourself." As Albertina became closer with Jackson, she also had a fortuitous meet-

"It is time for more people to know about legendary women like Albertina Walker and for them to get their due."

ing with Jackson's paper boy, a young James Cleveland, who would go on to become one of Albertina's closest friends and musical collaborators throughout her life.

Although she was the leader and manager of the Caravans, Albertina did not keep the microphone to herself. During the group's heyday, she shared leads, notably with Andrews and Caesar. By the mid-1950s, the Caravans began garnering a national audience, and soon they were setting a new standard for women in gospel music. "Albertina was not a stage hog," noted Tim Dillinger, gospel historian and independent researcher. "When she put her groups together, it was almost like cooking to put in the right ingredients, or in Albertina's case, the right singers, to make the best group."

Albertina and the Caravans were truly revolutionizing gospel music by having so many notable soloists in a single group. Albertina's commitment to ensuring that every voice in the group had time to shine eventually propelled many singers from the group to their

own successful groups and solo careers. Albertina was also one of the first people to vet a then unknown James Cleveland on one of his first recordings, "Ol' Time Religion." In fact, she believed in his talent so much that she refused to record an album without him when the executives at the Caravans' label at the time balked at Cleveland's gravelly voice and delivery. Little did they know that Albertina was refining and shaping one of the fathers of modern-day gospel.

By the late 1970s, Albertina began recording as a solo artist and created more than sixty albums throughout her career. Some of her gold-selling hits included "Please Be Patient with Me," "I Can Go to God in Prayer," and "Joy Will Come." Albertina's groundbreaking leadership and star-making power also led to her being a cofounder of the Gospel Music Workshop of America with Cleveland.

In 2006, Albertina reunited with the Caravans for what would become their gold-selling triumphant return titled *Paved the Way*. The group was back on top of the gospel charts like they had never left.

"When you talk about the music industry, it is dominated by men, controlled by men, the money is made by men, and the names that we know are primarily of men," said the Reverend Barbara Riley, an accomplished pastor and songwriter of the gospel hit "I Hear the Music in the Air," with Vickie Winans. "It is time for more people to know about legendary women like Albertina Walker and for them to get their due."

Willie Mae Ford Smith

Born: June 23, 1904
Died: February 2, 1994
Hometown: Rolling Fork, Mississippi
Notable Gospel Hits: "I'm Bound for Canaan Land," "If You Just Keep Still," "What Manner of Man Is This," "Going On with the Spirit"
Awards and Accolades: Known as the mother of gospel music, director of education for the National Convention of Gospel Choirs and Choruses for seventeen years, mentored several gospel greats including Mahalia Jackson, awarded the National Heritage Fellowship by the National Endowment of the Arts (1988).

When you spend more than sixty years of your life behind the scenes shaping, molding, and defining the sound of gospel music, it's hard to imagine having a renaissance in your career in your late eighties. But that's just what happened to Mother Willie Mae Ford Smith, who became the breakout star of the 1983 documentary *Say Amen, Somebody.* Throughout the film, she shows her dynamic gift for building and directing choirs, mentoring soloists, and infusing each song with precision and soul. At the film's climax, Smith is at the height of her powers, clad in a cream-colored suit and a diamond-encrusted cross, spinning the hymn "I'm Bound for Canaan Land" from a slow burn to a Holy Ghost furnace. She was so enraptured with the song that she had to be walked back to her seat, and she sat down with an exuberant exhaustion from her praise to God. She said at the film's conclusion, "Gospel music is just a feeling and you can't help yourself. I often feel like I'm going to fly away. I forget that I'm in the world sometimes and I just want to take off."

Willie Mae initially found her wings as a gospel singer growing up in Memphis, Tennessee. As one of fourteen children born to Clarence, a railroad brakeman, and Mary, a restaurant owner, she got her first inklings of the soul of gospel music from her maternal grandmother, a former slave, who she remembers singing, clapping, and doing the "Rock Daniel," her name for the holy dance.

The family moved to St. Louis when Willie Mae turned eleven, and she began singing in a quartet with three of her sisters, Mary, Emma, and Geneva, in 1922. Their first performance was at the National Baptist Convention, and they mesmerized the audience with the traditional hymn "Ezekiel Saw the Wheel." She and her sisters performed throughout the church circuit until each of her sisters married. Willie Mae became a solo artist two years later in 1924. During that same time, she married James Peter Smith, and they had two children, Willie James and Jacquelyn.

When Willie Mae branched out as a soloist, she had a fortuitous meeting with Thomas Dorsey, who became known as the father of gospel music. Dorsey began his musical career as a sideman for blues legend Bessie Smith before he devoted his life to gospel music. This dynamic duo of Willie Mae and Dorsey would go on to spark the creation of the National Convention of Gospel Choirs and Choruses (NCGCC). Willie Mae became the first director of education and headed the Soloists' Bureau for the organization.

As her role grew within the NCGCC, Willie Mae also became an ordained minister in her late twenties. Although it was deeply frowned upon for women to be ministers at that time, she became a dynamic force, combining the preached word with gospel music. She was originally ordained as a Methodist minister and then served as a pastor of Baptist churches in both Cincinnati and East St. Louis. She often said, "I don't understand why they didn't want women preaching. If a woman is nice enough to cook your food, make your bed, and clean your house, and care for your children, how come she can't carry the word out into the world?"

Willie Mae was known as a model of vocal delivery and performance strategy. She became legendary for her robust style and unique arrangements of old hymns and standards.

Willie Mae carried her fervor for the preached word into her singing career for the next two decades, as she made concert appearances and performed at church revivals. She was the first gospel performer to use a combination of introductory sermons and songs to open her performances. This style would be replicated by many women gospel singers over the years, including Dorothy Norwood and Shirley Caesar. "Gospel is just like the Christian Blues," she said in a rare 1973 interview. "I'm like a blues singer; when something's rubbing me wrong, I sing out my soul to settle me down."

For most of her career, Willie Mae was known as a model of vocal delivery and performance strategy. She became legendary for her robust style and unique arrangements of old hymns and standards. Willie Mae trained many gospel singers, including an up-and-coming Mahalia Jackson. She met Jackson when she was only thirty years old and still working as a hairdresser. They became close friends, and Willie Mae took an active hand in shaping Jackson's voice. Most of Willie Mae's life and influence in the gospel industry was lived behind the scenes until her sixties, when she recorded her first two albums, *I Believe I'll Run On* and *Going with the Spirit*.

Willie Mae was incredibly humble in her role in shaping numerous gospel singers and would have remained largely unknown outside the church walls had it not been for the creators of *Say Amen, Somebody* shaping a large portion of the film around her incredible accomplishments. After this dynamic performance, she was hailed as "one of the most important gospel singers of the century" by the *New York Times*.

After the film's tremendous reception, Willie Mae was awarded the National Heritage Fellowship by the National Endowment for the Arts in 1988. In one of her final interviews, Willie Mae shared, "When I first started singing gospel, the churches didn't want it. They said don't bring that coon-shine music in here. We don't want that ragtime singing in here. But that didn't stop me. I kept going because that is where God wanted the gospel and song." Willie Mae's humble roots and indelible imprint on gospel music will continue to fly high.

2

The Clark Sisters perform at the Seventh Annual Super Bowl Gospel Celebration.

SISTERS IN SONG

The Davis Sisters

Group Members and Birth Dates:
Ruth Davis, September 27, 1927–January 2, 1970
Thelma Davis, April 1, 1929–January 2, 1956
Audrey Davis, November 28, 1932–July 25, 1982
Alfreda Davis, January 1, 1934–June 15, 1990
Edna Davis, 1924–1977
Hometown: Philadelphia, Pennsylvania
Notable Gospel Hits: "Too Close to Heaven," "Surely God Is Able," "Jesus Steps Right In," "Bye and Bye," "Twelve Gates to the City," "Jesus, He's My King"
Awards and Accolades: The first female group to sing "hard" gospel—pioneering a unique physical style with highly emotive synchronized harmonies and choreographed movements. Mentored and influenced by Gertrude Ward of the Famous Clara Ward Singers. Recorded prolifically for many labels and were popular around the world. Their 1968 hit "Wait a Little Longer" was nominated for a Grammy.

The Davis Sisters: Ruth, Thelma, Audrey, and Alfreda Davis along with Curtis Dublin.

When you need some double-hand-clapping and tambourine-swinging harmonies, the Davis Sisters from Philadelphia are sure to deliver. Just one listen of their most prolific hit, "Twelve Gates to the City," and you are immediately transported into the spirit of a good old-fashioned Sunday night service. Mentored by Gertrude Ward, mother of gospel legend Clara Ward and mastermind behind the Famous Clara Ward Singers, the Davis Sisters—Ruth, Thelma, Audrey, Alfreda, and Edna—followed their blueprint to wide acclaim throughout the country.

The Davis Sisters began singing together at Philadelphia's Mount Zion Fire Baptized Holiness Church. In the mid-1940s, the oldest sister, Ruth, organized her sisters into an ensemble in their teens. They recruited their cousin Curtis to be their pianist, and the sisters hit the chitlin circuit with great success in the late 1940s and early 1950s. The sisters soon became known as an edgier version of the Clara Ward Singers.

"The Davis Sisters were one of the first gospel groups who came out of the Holiness Church," noted Tim Dillinger, gospel historian and independent researcher. "The holiness tradition gave them more freedom to sing harder, speak in tongues, lay out on the ground when they were swept up in to the spirit. Legend has it that they would sing so hard that at the end of their performances, they would say to each other, 'Girl, you peed tonight!'"

The sisters became known as the first female group to sing "hard gospel." Their style was so dynamic that they often intimidated male groups. This style was described as highly emotive, filled with synchronized harmonies, and punctuated with choreographed movements. They positioned themselves onstage around a central microphone to emulate the sound of a small choir. Robert Sacre wrote in the *Encyclopedia of American Gospel Music*, "The Davis Sisters were the first female group to sing the 'hard' gospel that was totally different from the Baptist style of singing, which emphasized beauty of tone, precise rhythm,

The sound and precision of the Davis Sisters was so beloved, that Ray Charles designed his background singers, the Raelettes, after their signature sound.

and occasional ornamentation; hard gospel was characterized by straining the voice during periods of spiritual ecstasy, singing at the extremes of ranges, repeating words or syllables, adding lots of interjections, and 'acting out' songs with motions, stoops, and movements."

As the group began to gain popularity throughout Philadelphia, Gertrude Ward took an interest in the sisters, helped them to refine their style, and assisted them with procuring their first recording contract. The Davis Sisters recorded their first two singles on the Apex label in May 1949. The group also recorded on Gotham Records before finding a permanent home at Savoy Records in 1955. Their first session for Savoy yielded the Davis Sisters' biggest hit, "Twelve Gates to the City."

Many of the group's musical arrangements were developed by Ruth, who incorporated sounds from doo-wop, R&B, and emerging rock and roll songs of the time. Although considered controversial in gospel music, Ruth

wasn't afraid to bring new sounds into the group to bring new flavor into the gospel music arena. "Ruth was the hardest female belter in gospel, 'scared of no man' when it came to squalling," Anthony Heilbut observed in his book *The Gospel Sound: Good News and Hard Times*. "At home she'd enthrall friends with her blues, and all the singers insist she could have been another Dinah Washington or Big Maybelle."

The sound and precision of the Davis Sisters was so beloved that Ray Charles designed his background singers, the Raelettes, after their signature sound. The Davis Sisters were also a huge influence on gospel legend Richard Smallwood, who first heard their music at the tender age of six.

"I believe that the Davis Sisters' true legacy is providing a blueprint for a divine union of Gospel and the Blues," Dillinger said. "You could always count on them to be authentic in their humanity and be true in their imperfections."

Tensions within the group splintered their unity in the early sixties, but not before they delivered one final album, *I Believe I'll Go Back Home*. This was the final recording before Ruth died an untimely death at age forty-two. "All the songs on that album were focused on heaven and completing the journey," Dillinger shared. "It was almost like Ruth was giving her final goodbyes and standing in her prophetic greatness." The Davis Sisters' legacy lives with their recordings and many women gospel groups who have emulated their timeless sound.

The Barrett Sisters

Group Members and Birth Dates:
Delois Barrett Campbell, March 12, 1926–August 2, 2011
Billie Barrett GreenBey, birth date unknown,
1928–February 28, 2020
Rodessa Barrett Porter, birth date unknown, 1930
(last surviving sister)
Hometown: Chicago, Illinois
Notable Gospel Hits: "Jesus Loves Me," "I'll Fly Away,"
"Carry Me Back," "God So Loved the World," "The Storm
Is Passing Over," "Coming Again So Soon"
Awards and Accolades: Considered the world's greatest
female trio in gospel history, producing a plethora of
recordings and bringing gospel music to nations on nearly
every continent. Named American goodwill ambassadors
during the 1980s. Their name, "The Barrett Sisters," is
engraved on the prestigious Stellar Awards, presented
annually for gospel music achievements.

The Barrett Sisters.

When Delois, Billie, and Rodessa Barrett open their mouths to sing God's praises, heaven is sure to show up in the room. This anointed trio was known for swooping their voices from octave to octave and singing together in perfect harmony. From Rodessa's first soprano to Delois's second soprano to Billie holding down the harmony with her brilliant alto, the Barrett Sisters performed around the globe for more than sixty years and electrified audiences with their sweet tones that regularly brought sold-out crowds to their feet.

The Barrett Sisters were the Chicago version of their New Jersey counterparts, the Drinkard Singers. The sisters grew up on Chicago's South Side and were members of the Morning Star Baptist Church. They sang in the choir under the direction of their aunt, who often taught the sisters songs from the father of gospel, Thomas Dorsey. The Barrett Sisters grew their skills in the same talented pot of gospel singers that hailed from Chicago; both Dorsey and Mahalia Jackson were close friends and neighbors of the trio.

Delois, the oldest sister and the group's eventual leader, began her professional career as a first soprano with the Roberta Martin Singers in the 1940s. Delois and Billie also performed with their cousins in a group called the Barrett-Hudson Singers. Billie also trained as a student at the American Conservatory of Music, and Rodessa was a director for the Galilee Baptist Church Choir.

As the different groups that the sisters sang with split and branched out, the sisters came together in the early 1960s to form their own group. The Barrett Sisters recorded their first album, *Jesus Loves Me*, in 1963. Their later albums included *I'll Fly Away* and *Carry Me Back* for Savoy and in the 1970s *God So Loved the World* and *Coming Again So Soon* on the Creed label. The Barrett Sisters soon became a fixture on the Chicago gospel scene, and they often appeared on *Jubilee Showcase*, a local television show that featured the nation's top gospel groups. "We're not ministers, and we're not preachers," Billie told the *Wisconsin State Journal* in 1990, "but we're singing about the good news and the good times happening with the Lord."

Similar to gospel great Willie Mae Ford Smith, the sisters gained a new wave of fans after being featured in the film *Say Amen, Somebody.* The group's stirring performances of "The Storm Is Passing Over," "(I Don't Feel) No Ways Tired," and "He Has Brought Us" were highlights of the film. Rodessa said in an interview with ABC 7 in August 2019: "We felt these songs. I mean, it just wasn't singing. We believed in them, we felt them. The gospel music in our hearts will always live on."

After the documentary, the Barrett Sisters were invited to sing on *The Tonight Show*, *The Oprah Winfrey Show*, and *Bobby Jones Gospel*. In their later years, the sisters were also featured in a 2013 documentary called *The Sweet Sisters of Zion.*

Delois beautifully summed up the sisters' legacy in this 1990 *Chicago Tribune* article: "I suppose gospel music came into being because we black people, as a race, had been crushed so much, and so cruelly. So these gospel songs of ours were comforting and consoling to us. I believe that the people who wrote the first gospel songs were inspired by God to write, to give our people something to feed on or to live on."

The Clark Sisters

Group Members and Birth Dates:
Jacky Clark-Chisholm, December 29, 1948
Elbernita "Twinkie" Clark, November 15, 1954
Dorinda Clark-Cole, October 19, 1957
Karen Clark-Sheard, November 15, 1960
Denise Clark-Bradford, birth date unknown
Hometown: Detroit, Michigan
Notable Gospel Hits: "Is My Living in Vain?," "Expect Your Miracle," "Hallelujah"
Notable Crossover Hits: "You Brought the Sunshine," "Name It, Claim It"
Awards and Accolades: Bestselling female gospel group of all time, one Dove Award, three Grammy Awards, James Cleveland Lifetime Achievement Award (2020, Thirty-Fifth Annual Stellar Awards)

The Clark Sisters performing onstage at
Royalty Theatre, London, August 27, 1989.

Recording artists Karen Clark-Sheard (*left*) and Donnie McClurkin perform onstage during the 2016 Stellar Gospel Awards at the Orleans Arena on February 20, 2016, in Las Vegas, Nevada.

During the 1985 Grammy Awards, the Clark Sisters had exactly two minutes to show the world why they belonged onstage during the biggest night in music. But 120 seconds was more than enough time for Jacky, Twinkie, Dorinda, Karen, and their mother, the legendary Dr. Mattie Moss Clark, to electrify the auditorium with their signature harmonies and world-class sound. The Clark Sisters and Dr. Clark burst onto the stage in head-to-toe black sequins and blooming feathered headpieces. From the moment baby sister Karen belted out, "Clap your hands and praise him!" in her signature soprano voice, the Clark Sisters were officially catapulted from the church to the global stage.

Just a few years earlier, the Clark Sisters were light-years from sequins and feathers, as they were still discovering how to honor their Christian roots in the Church of God in Christ and emerge as women in gospel music who were poised to redefine the genre. As the Clark Sisters were developing, honing, and refining what would be later called "the Clark

Snoop Dogg performs with Jacky Clark-Chisholm, Dorinda Clark-Cole, and Karen Clark-Sheard of the Clark Sisters onstage during BET Presents Nineteenth Annual Super Bowl Gospel Celebration at Bethel University on February 1, 2018, in St. Paul, Minnesota.

(left to right) Jacky Clark-Chisholm, Dorinda Clark, and Karen Clark-Sheard of the Clark Sisters perform at the Dell Music Center on August 2, 2012, in Philadelphia, Pennsylvania.

Sound," the foundation that undergirded everything for them was their deep bond as a family. "The thing that truly kept the Clark Sisters going was their pure camaraderie as sisters," said Larry Clark, a minister, musician, and son of founding member Denise Clark-Bradford.

That strong family foundation began under the genius and tutelage of their mother. Dr. Clark was a legend in gospel music, the first choir director to record a choir with three-part harmony, and many of the three hundred compositions that she recorded throughout her life went on to become standard hymnals in the Black church. She and daughter Twinkie were pioneers of incorporating drums and electric guitars and bass into the modern-day worship experience. The Clark Sisters often toured the country with their mother as she conducted choir workshops and revivals with the Church of God in Christ.

Larry Clark, who took care of his grandmother in her later years, shared that she kept an enormous collection of cassette tapes under

After nearly fifty years, the sky is the limit for the message that the Clark Sisters bring and the hearts that they have touched all over the world.

her queen-size bed that were filled with early, unfinished recordings by her and her daughters. "My grandmother's devotion to her faith, her music, and her daughters was out of this world," Clark said.

As the Clark Sisters emerged from under their mother's wings, they signed their first record deal in 1973 and released their first album, *Jesus Has a Lot to Give*. Throughout the 1970s, the sisters electrified churchgoers throughout the country with gospel hits such as "Is My Living in Vain?," "Pure Gold," and "Expect Your Miracle." Before the release of their 1981 album *You Brought the Sunshine*, Twinkie, also known as "the Queen of the Hammond B-3 Organ," took charge of the group's songwriting and vocal arrangements. With the debut of this album, the Clark Sisters scored their first crossover hit, "You Brought the Sunshine," which gained popularity on both gospel and secular stations.

Throughout the late 1980s and 1990s, the Clark Sisters continued to minister to audiences throughout the globe with both group

(left to right) Shelea Frazier, Christina Bell, Kierra Sheard, Angela Birchett, and Raven Goodwin perform live onstage following Lifetime's panel "The Clark Sisters: First Ladies of Gospel" during the A&E Networks TCA 2020 Winter Press Tour at the Langham Huntington, in Pasadena, California.

and solo albums, and they mesmerized their listeners with gospel classics such as "Jesus Is a Love Song," "Pray for the USA," and "Name It, Claim It."

In the late 1990s and early 2000s, the Clark Sisters branched out into solo careers. Karen Clark-Sheard collaborated with Donald Lawrence to produce four bestselling gospel albums and earned numerous Stellar Awards as a solo artist. Jazzy-voiced Dorinda Clark-Cole emerged in her own right as "the Rose of Gospel," with three solo albums, and is known for her electric performances that feature her preaching and singing ministry. Sisters Jacky and Twinkie have also produced solo albums, and Twinkie and Larry Clark debuted a duet album in 2020 called *Generations* that features never-before-heard recordings from Dr. Clark. The next generation of the Clark family includes Karen's daughter, Kierra, who has become gospel royalty in her own right, with several Stellar Awards and gold gospel albums under her belt, and Karen's son, J. Drew, who is a drummer and frequent producer for the Clark Sisters.

The Clark Sisters perform at the funeral service for Aretha Franklin at the Greater Grace Temple in Detroit, Michigan, August 31, 2018.

The Clark Sisters could have rested on their fame and legacy, but in 2007, they came back together and recorded their first group album in more than a decade, scoring two Grammy Awards for the song "Blessed and Highly Favored" and the album *Live: One Last Time*. During this live recording, you could feel the electricity in the room as the sisters sang their most beloved hits and introduced a new generation to their classic sound.

In 2020, they gained a new legion of fans after their Lifetime movie *The Clark Sisters: First Ladies of Gospel* became the highest debut on the network, with 2.7 million viewers. After nearly fifty years, the sky is the limit for the message that the Clark Sisters bring and the hearts that they have touched all over the world.

Clara Ward and the Ward Singers

Born: April 21, 1924
Died: January 16, 1973
Hometown: Philadelphia, Pennsylvania
Notable Gospel Hits: "Surely, God Is Able," "How I Got Over," "Packin' Up"
Awards and Accolades: One of the first gospel groups to have multiple million-selling hits, Songwriters Hall of Fame (1977)

American gospel singer and pianist Clara Ward (1924–1973) in a recording studio, Copenhagen, Denmark, September 1970.

When Clara Ward and the Ward Singers appeared on *The Flip Wilson Show* in 1971, they had the elegance, grace, and poise of the Supremes, but the sound coming from their lips was a lot more heavenly. The Ward Singers electrified that stage with tambourines swinging, an organ thrumming, and their perfectly coiffed hair bouncing in time to the rhythm. The performance became so dynamic that one of the singers' tambourines broke at the end of the final song. Certainly *The Flip Wilson Show* was more suited to dignified performances, with the audience politely clapping at the end of the performance. But there was just no way that the incomparable Clara Ward could grace the stage without everyone in the room rising to their feet. This was far from the last time that Clara and the Ward Singers would enrapture a television audience with their exuberant praise and songs. "Clara Ward was a phenomenon. She knew how to work the aisles and give the audience a true show whenever she sang," said George Faison, legendary choreographer and collaborator with numerous gospel and R&B performers.

The Ward Singers' foot-stomping, soul-shaking, and tambourine-breaking performances began under the tutelage of the Wards' matriarch, Gertrude Mae Ward, in 1931 in their hometown of Philadelphia. Originally known as the Consecrated Gospel Singers, the group's first lineup included Gertrude, her oldest daughter, Willarene Mae, and a seven-year-old Clara holding the high notes. Gertrude soon became a master marketeer in showcasing the group's talent and garnering them steady performances.

Clara recorded her first solo record in 1940, and the group embarked on its first national tour in 1943. The group made headlines with a soul-stirring performance at the National Baptist Convention during their first year on tour. In the late 1940s, Henrietta Waddy and Marion Williams joined the group, and both singers brought a Pentecostal flair and delivery to round out the Ward Singers' sound.

"It was truly unbelievable what Clara could do with a song. She always brought Almighty God with her onstage, and every performance was an earth-shattering experience that no one could ever forget."

By the beginning of the 1950s, Clara and the group began touring with the Reverend C. L. Franklin, father of the queen of soul, Aretha Franklin. Ward and Franklin became close friends, and eventually Clara became one of Aretha's mentors and confidants. "Clara was clearly Aretha's biggest influence," said Tim Dillinger, gospel historian and independent researcher. "You could see it in everything from Aretha's phrasing in her songs, to the elegance of wearing furs and then removing it with a flourish, down to keeping her money and her pocketbook closely at her side."

By the end of the decade, Clara and the Famous Ward Singers, as they were now called, performed at Carnegie Hall and recorded three of the first million-selling singles in gospel music: "Surely God Is Able," "Move On Up a Little Higher," and their signature showstopper, "How I Got Over." What made the group's sound so infectious was their quartet style of switching leads between singers, which allowed the group to improvise songs in the moment and gave the singers the freedom to move their

Ward performs with the
Ward Singers, circa 1960s.

Ward in the recording
studio in Copenhagen,
Denmark, September 1970.

songs however the Holy Spirit led them to do so. Clara was also a prolific composer who set the standard for popular gospel compositions.

Clara and the Famous Ward Singers also became known for eschewing traditional choir robes in favor of glamorous gowns and hairdos that soared to the sky. "Clara and the Ward Singers brought style to gospel music. They were never shabby. They always had the best wigs, jewelry, clothes, and shoes," Faison said. With their polished style, Clara was able to take the Famous Ward Singers beyond the confines of the church walls and introduce gospel music into venues most gospel singers had never dared to venture.

It was a good thing that Clara encouraged the group to evolve beyond their gospel roots because just as the chitlin circuit began drying up in the early 1960s, the Famous Ward Singers were invited to perform in the club circuit in Las Vegas and Disney World, tour as an opening act for comedian Jack Benny, and star on Broadway in Langston Hughes's play *Tambourines to Glory*. The Famous Ward Singers also toured extensively overseas in Australia, Japan, Indonesia, Thailand, and throughout Europe. Clara also got a taste of Hollywood with a small supporting role in the film *A Time to Sing*. The group was also a cherished favorite on American variety shows such as *The Mike Douglas Show*, *The Ed Sullivan Show*, and *The Flip Wilson Show*. While Clara became extraordinarily wealthy for a Black woman of her era, many of her confidants at the time revealed that she was very lonely and found it hard to truly enjoy the fruits of her success.

Clara and the Famous Ward Singers continued to tour well into the early 1970s until Clara's health began to decline. One of her last public appearances was for the epic recording of Aretha Franklin's opus "Amazing Grace." While Clara's voice on earth came to a close in 1973, her voice lives on as a woman who was a true pioneer of the power of gospel music. "It was truly unbelievable what Clara could do with a song," Faison shared. "She always brought Almighty God with her onstage, and every performance was an earth-shattering experience that no one could ever forget."

Accompanist Robert Johnson *(center)* surrounded by gospel singers "the Ward Singers": *(left to right)* Edna James, Jessie Tucker, Gertrude Ward, Clara Ward, Dorothy Robinson, and Mildred Means, in London prior to embarking on their European tour, April 4, 1959.

The Drinkard Singers

Group Members and Birth Dates:
Emily "Cissy" Drinkard Houston, September 30, 1933
Lee Drinkard Warwick, 1920–2005
Anne Drinkard-Moss, 1927–2003
Nick Drinkard, 1929–1992
Larry Drinkard, 1931–2012
Hometown: Newark, New Jersey
Notable Gospel Hits: "Rise, Shine," "Lift Him Up,"
"Just a Little While to Stay Here," "My Faith Looks Up
to Thee"
Awards and Accolades: First gospel group to record
on a major label, RCA Records (1959)

Cissy Houston poses for
a studio portrait in 1977
in the United States.

An undated publicity photo of the Drinkard Singers. The pioneering group was based out of New Jersey.

After just one listen of the Drinkard Singers' rendition of "Rise, Shine," you can easily understand why Mahalia Jackson personally invited the group to be her opening act at the Newport Jazz Festival in 1957. You can hear a strong and commanding solo by the baby sister of the group, Emily, who would be better known in her career as the legendary Cissy Houston, that was perfectly paired with the tight and bright harmony of her siblings Lee, Nick, Anne, and Larry.

"It's often hard for me to find just the right words to express their sound, but the first word that I always think of is simply magnificent," said multiple Grammy winner and daughter of founding member Lee Drinkard, Dionne Warwick. "They were definitely inspired by God. It was the kind of sound that made people rise to their feet."

This Holy Ghost–filled and fire-baptized group began under the leadership of their father, Nicholas Drinkard. He was a tall, handsome man with distinguished gray eyes who served as a deacon at their home church, the New

After the Newport Jazz Festival, the Drinkard Singers became the first gospel group signed to RCA Records in 1959.

A young Whitney Houston *(center)* performs with her mother, Cissy Houston *(left)*, circa 1982 in New York City.

Hope Baptist Church in Newark, New Jersey. This group sang in perfect four-part harmony with Anne as soprano, Cissy as alto, Lee as first tenor, and brother Larry rounding out the sound as second tenor. "These were some of the first songs that I ever heard as a child," Warwick shared. "All of their songs were my favorite. They had their own sound."

Warwick recalls seeing her mother, her aunts, and her uncles rehearsing around the family's white baby grand piano at their home in Newark and performing at their home church. As she grew older, she was invited to sing with the group when they needed a substitute in the lineup. "It was a sensational experience to perform with them," Warwick said. "I felt honored that they thought I was good enough to sing with them. They were very serious about their craft."

One of the unique dynamics in the Drinkard Singers is that the women in the group took on equal footing with the men. Cissy and Anne were the group's primary songwriters, and Lee served as the group's manager. "It was good for me to see them in leadership roles," War-

A young Whitney Houston *(right)* poses with her mother, Cissy Houston, circa 1982 in West Orange, New Jersey.

wick noted. "This highly influenced me later on in my career. I was confident enough to sign all of my checks and make decisions for myself."

After the Newport Jazz Festival, the Drinkard Singers became the first gospel group signed to RCA Records in 1959. On the cover of their first album, *Joyful Noise*, the siblings wear bright gold robes as they sing their praises to God. By 1967, the group became the legendary R&B group the Sweet Inspirations, and they sang background vocals for Aretha Franklin, Elvis Presley, and niece Dionne Warwick.

Warwick concluded that she believed that being in the presence of her family's singing tradition provided her with a rich training ground. She hopes that other women in gospel music will follow in her family's footsteps and that "other women will learn to always be dedicated to their craft, have a strong belief in what they do, and always honor God. These are the qualities that I believe make a true gospel singer." With this firm legacy in place, the Drinkard Singers will no doubt continue to be one of the pivotal bricks in the foundation of gospel music.

Cissy Houston at the New Orleans Jazz Festival.

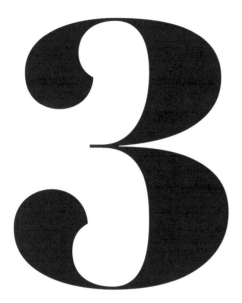

3

ARCHITECTS
OF THE MELODY

Dorothy Love Coates

Born: January 30, 1928

Died: April 9, 2002

Hometown: Birmingham, Alabama

Notable Gospel Hits: "I'm Sealed," "Get Away Jordan," "That's Enough," "He's Right on Time," "Heaven," "I Won't Let Go," "Ninety-Nine and a Half Won't Do," "You Must Be Born Again"

Awards and Accolades: During her fifty-year career, Dorothy wrote and recorded more than three hundred songs and recorded twenty albums. A documentary about her life called *Still Holding On: The Music of Dorothy Love Coates and the Original Gospel Harmonettes* earned an Emmy in 2000 (produced by Dwight Cammeron). The prestigious Dorothy Love Coates Living Legend Award is presented annually by the American Gospel Quartet Convention.

Dorothy Love Coates at the 1979 New Orleans Jazz Festival.

If you want to understand the true foundation of gospel music, you have to start with Dorothy Love Coates. Just listening to Dorothy and her group the Gospel Harmonettes singing "He's Right on Time," you can hear her influence on everyone from Aretha Franklin to Mavis Staples to rock pioneer Little Richard. Known for her rough delivery and gravelly voice, Dorothy was one of the greatest performers of gospel music, and she regularly stirred crowds into a frenzy with her intense vocalizations and animated style. Dorothy was also known for outsinging most of her male gospel counterparts of the time.

Born Dorothy McGriff in Birmingham, Alabama, she began playing the piano at the Evergreen Baptist Church at the age of ten, and then joined her sisters and brothers in the family group, the McGriff Singers, during her teenage years. She dropped out of school in tenth grade to support her family, working as a maid and a clerk. In a 1965 interview she said, "On weekdays I work for the white man. On the weekends I sing for the people."

She married her first husband, Willie Love, in 1946. He was the lead of one of the most popular quartets in gospel music at the time. One year later, Dorothy became the lead singer and songwriter for the Birmingham all-female group the Gospel Harmonettes, and wrote most of the music. The Gospel Harmonettes recorded their first hit, "I'm Sealed," in 1951. Over the years the group recorded on RCA, Specialty Records, Nashboro, and Vee-Jay labels. Some of the group's hits included "You Must Be Born Again" and "That's Enough" on the Specialty label, "I Won't Let Go of My Faith" on Nashboro, and "You've Been Good to Me" on Vee-Jay.

Dorothy and the Gospel Harmonettes toured throughout the United States and the Bahamas, and they performed at Carnegie Hall, the Apollo Theater, and Madison Square Garden. Dorothy was the architect behind the group's success. She often sang with such a high spirit that members of the group would have to lead her off the stage. An up-and-coming James Brown would go on to copy Love's performance style and her delivery throughout his career. Over the years, some of the most prolific members of the group included Evelyn Starks Hardy, a talented and mesmerizing pianist; Mildred Madison Miller, a mezzo-soprano with a southern flair; Odessa Edwards, an alto with tremendous power and soul; and Vera Conner Kilb, a first soprano who delivered high notes that were often imitated but never duplicated. Dorothy incorporated mini-sermons throughout her performances and shared her views on the world at large before mesmerizing the audience with song. By the early 1960s, the group had a regular half-hour radio show.

Dorothy was active in the civil rights movement. As she frequently toured throughout the country, she was an active participant in many marches with Dr. Martin Luther King Jr. and worked on voter registration drives, and many of her songs in the latter part of her career openly criticized racial discrimination and segregation throughout the Jim Crow South.

She also performed at numerous benefit concerts and civil rights rallies and was often arrested for her activism.

While many of her gospel contemporaries went on to have thriving careers, Dorothy grew bitter toward the end of her life because of her fervent stance on staying committed to gospel music and not crossing over to secular fame. "They told me I had to stop singing gospel and cross over to make a dollar," she told a Birmingham newspaper in her later years. "I wouldn't do it. I decided to stay with my maker. There's nowhere else we can go but to the Lord."

While Dorothy may not have received proper recognition during her lifetime, there's not a gospel singer alive who would not agree that she set the standard for being a gospel singer infused with soul, integrity, and a firm mission to make sure that her people were properly represented in song.

Dorothy Norwood

Born: May 29, 1935

Hometown: Atlanta, Georgia

Notable Gospel Hits: "The Denied Mother," "Shake the Devil Off," "The Storm Is Almost Gone"

Awards and Accolades: Five Gold Albums, numerous Dove, Grammy, and Stellar Award nominations

Nominee Dorothy Norwood attends the 2016 Stellar Gospel Awards at the Orleans Arena on February 20, 2016, in Las Vegas, Nevada.

When you hear the steady beat of the tambourine and the warm humming of the organ in Dorothy Norwood's classic "The Denied Mother," you can't help but feel like you are in a southern tent revival in the middle of a summer evening. Norwood's strong alto voice takes the congregation through a triumphant testimony of a mother who overcomes the impossible to raise her daughter and crescendos into a fiery call-and-response version of "Precious Lord, Take My Hand" with her talented background singers. While this song is nearly thirteen minutes long, you still want to hear Norwood croon and bring forth the good news of the gospel a little while longer.

"Dorothy Norwood is one of those gospel singers who sung out of her gut," shared the Reverend Barbara Riley, an accomplished pastor and songwriter of the gospel hit "I Hear the Music in the Air" with Vickie Winans. "I had a teacher who didn't like gospel music because she said it sounded like the gutter. I disagreed with her because, in truth, that's what singers like Dorothy Norwood were trying to do—sing their way out of the gutter."

Known throughout the gospel industry as "the World's Greatest Storyteller," Dorothy is a full-bodied, down-home singer and a preacher who can take you from the depths of the most challenging situations in the human experience, and by the end of her concerts you are *sho nuff* reminded of God's promise to heal, transform, and deliver. Young Dorothy began her musical journey with her family at the tender age of eight in her hometown of Atlanta, Georgia. She was awarded a scholarship to Morris Brown College, and after completing her degree, she had a dream about becoming a gospel singer and moving to Chicago. That dream came to fruition in 1956 when she moved to Chicago and began singing with the legendary Mahalia Jackson and the Reverend James Cleveland. She caught Jackson's ear at the Forty-Fourth Street Baptist Church when someone sent a note to Jackson that Dorothy was in the room and that she could blow. Dorothy indeed blew Jackson away, and the legendary singer invited a young Dorothy on the road with her for six months. After touring with Jackson, Dorothy returned to Chicago and joined the Reverend Clay Evans's church and became a featured soloist with the hymn "Low Is the Way." She became so loved for that solo that the church members started calling her "Low."

Soon Dorothy caught the ear of the Caravans' founder, Albertina Walker, and became part of the dynamic lineup that included Shirley Caesar and Inez Andrews. Before she was recruited, Dorothy was working at a hamburger shack making thirty dollars a week. So when the offer came to sing with the Caravans for thirty dollars a night, she was grateful for the opportunity to use her gift for the glory of God.

What began setting Dorothy apart was her keen ability to tell a good story with each song. "Many women gospel singers used their platforms to express themselves as the natural preachers that they were," Riley said.

When Dorothy's solo career took off in 1964, she was more than ready to share her gift of both the preached word and a powerful message through song. Her first album, *Johnny & Jesus*, was certified gold, and her follow-up record, *A Denied Mother*, became an instant classic, with its hopeful message of encouragement to Black mothers everywhere. Dorothy's career soon soared beyond the church walls, as she was invited to be the opening act for the Rolling Stones for a thirty-city US tour in 1972.

Dorothy has successfully released more than two dozen albums on the Malaco and Savoy gospel labels, including a gold-selling reunion album with the Caravans in 2006. She has continued to top the gospel charts and has become a staple for many gospel concerts and tours. Much like her Caravan sister, the Reverend Shirley Caesar, Dorothy shows no signs of slowing down and gives her audience exactly what they want—more of her classic stories and songs about the good news of Jesus.

Marion Williams

Born: August 29, 1927
Died: July 2, 1994
Hometown: Miami, Florida
Notable Gospel Hits: "Surely, God Is Able," "Standing Here Wondering Which Way to Go," "Packin' Up," "How I Got Over," "The Day Is Past and Gone"
Awards and Accolades: Recipient of a lifetime achievement award at the Kennedy Center Honors (1993), first singer and gospel artist to receive a MacArthur Foundation "genius" grant (1993), inducted into the Philadelphia Walk of Fame (1994), her album *Prayer Changes Things* won a Grand Prix du Disque in France (1976). Her recording of "How I Got Over" sold more than a million copies. Served as a musical ambassador for the US State Department.

American gospel singer Marion Williams (August 29, 1927–July 2, 1994) in 1962. Marion was a protégée of Clara Ward and the Famous Ward Singers, a seminal gospel group in the 1950s. Pursuing a solo career, Marion's gospel stylings inspired other gospel-influenced contemporary singers including Little Richard and Aretha Franklin. Marion was the recipient in 1993 of the prestigious MacArthur "genius" grant.

To hear Marion Williams's powerful voice at the climax of her signature hit "Packin' Up" is the equivalent of experiencing electric joy in motion. During one of her televised performances of this song, the legendary singer became so ignited with her praise that she almost lost her clip-on ponytail in the process. Marion became known for reaching the highest heights of her soprano range and turning any gospel song into a solid gold hit. "When I'm singing, I get inspired by God," she said in a 1980 interview with the *New York Times*. "I call it 'the anointing.' It's an extra-special thing. When the inspiration of God is missing, I just rely on talent."

This southern girl was born in Miami, Florida, one of eleven children, and was one of only three of her siblings who made it past their first year of life. She began singing at the age of three at the local Church of God and was inspired by Sister Rosetta Tharpe and the Smith Jubilee Singers. By the time Marion became a teenager, she was singing on the weekends in storefront churches and revivals, and she gained a reputation as a top soloist throughout Miami. Marion was a constant student of several genres of music, including jazz, opera, and blues, but her heart was always set on becoming a gospel singer. "I don't have nothing against other people and what they do, but I don't want no part of singing secular music," she said in a 1993 interview. "I was offered one hundred thousand dollars to make one blues record, and I turned it down. I sing for the Lord, and that's enough for me."

Marion's great vocal range was recognized by Clara and Gertrude Ward when she was visiting her sister in Philadelphia in 1946. A year later, Marion joined the Ward Singers and became one of their lead soloists. Her first song with the group was "How Far Am I from Canaan" in 1948 and was soon followed up by the hit "Surely God Is Able." This song skyrocketed the group into fame throughout the gospel arena. Marion was a star attraction in the Ward Singers until her departure in 1958.

From the Ward Singers, Marion moved on to perform with the Stars of Faith. The group recorded for Savoy and Charlie records. The Stars of Faith found huge success with an appearance in the Broadway musical *Black Nativity* in 1961, written by the incomparable Langston Hughes. The play featured an all-Black cast and was the first Broadway musical to incorporate gospel music.

"Marion was truly a song stylist," said Tim Dillinger, gospel historian and independent researcher. "Each of her concerts was an experience where she never replicated her sound, and the audience was always mesmerized because you never knew where she would take a song."

After the whirlwind success of *Black Nativity*, Marion embarked on a solo career. She toured throughout the United States, Europe, and Africa in the 1960s. She became so popular that the US State Department sponsored her tour of Africa in 1966. Throughout the late 1960s and 1970s, Marion recorded for several labels, including Epic, Columbia, and Savoy. She scored huge hits with the singles "Wondering," "Someone Bigger Than You and I," and "Holy Ghost Don't Leave Me." "Marion's goal was always to reach outside the walls," Dillinger shared. Her expansive reach led to more than a dozen solo albums, and she was a guest soloist in 1992 for the Lincoln Center's Avery Fisher Hall premiere of Wynton Marsalis's gospel-influenced jazz suite *In This House, On This Morning*.

When Marion was honored by the MacArthur Foundation in 1993, the foundation noted that she was among "the last surviving links to gospel's golden age . . . one of the most versatile singers of her generation."

Pastor Shirley Caesar

Born: October 13, 1938
Hometown: Durham, North Carolina
Notable Gospel Hits: "No Charge," "Don't Drive Your Mama Away," "Satan, We're Gonna Tear Your Kingdom Down"
Notable Crossover Hits: "Hold My Mule," "I Remember Mama," "Jesus, I Love Calling Your Name"
Awards and Accolades: Twelve Grammy Awards, Grammy Lifetime Achievement Award, fourteen Stellar Awards, eighteen Dove Awards, NAACP Lifetime Achievement Award

Singer Shirley Caesar performs onstage during the 2011 BET Awards held at the Shrine Auditorium on June 26, 2011, in Los Angeles, California.

Singer Shirley Caesar performs onstage during the 2013 BET Celebration of Gospel at Orpheum Theatre on March 16, 2013, in Los Angeles, California.

When you come in the presence of Pastor Shirley Caesar, you better get ready for a Holy Ghost good time. While this powerful evangelist is only five foot one, her voice commands the power of God in every room where she stands, and she has been using that powerful voice to spread the good news of Jesus Christ for more than sixty years.

"Shirley Caesar has been one of the most influential singers in my life," said the Reverend Barbara Riley, an accomplished pastor and songwriter of the gospel hit "I Hear the Music in the Air" with Vickie Winans. "The grit in which she sang, the soul-wrenching sound of her music, always reached me. The words that she sings are always sung out of the heart, out of the spirit, and out of experience. How her music comes to you and saturates you gets you into places where the preached word can't. Even if you can't remember every word of a song, you will remember the peace that touched your soul."

Shirley, a native of Durham, North Carolina, has been singing gospel music since she was four years old. As the tenth child of her large family of twelve siblings, she joined the Just Came Four, a quartet led by her father, James, when she was ten years old. Shirley recorded her first single, "I'd Rather Have Jesus," at age thirteen.

As Shirley continued developing her gift throughout her teenage years, she noted that she definitively heard the voice of God calling her to ministry during a typing class at North Carolina Central University. Soon after she heard God's voice, Shirley discovered that there was an opening for the legendary Caravans from Chicago, and she sent in an audition tape.

Pastor Caesar soon became part of the legendary lineup with the Caravans that also included Inez Andrews, Albertina Walker, Dorothy Norwood, and Sara McKissick. Some of Shirley's most powerful solos with the group included her scorching rendition of "I Won't Be Back" and the heart-wrenching "Don't Drive Mama Away."

Recording artist Shirley Caesar attends a ceremony honoring her with a star on the Hollywood Walk of Fame on June 28, 2016, in Hollywood, California.

"Back then, women were not looked upon favorably as preachers. So to get a message across you had to pack it into a song for it to be received, not only by men, but by women in the congregation as well," Riley shared. "The sermon had to be cloaked in the song, otherwise people would not listen. They were also trying to express themselves as the natural preachers that they were."

Songs like "No Charge," "I Remember Mama," and "Don't Drive Mama Away" spoke deeply to the relationships between mother and child and how those dynamics were beginning to change in American society. Songs like that were trying to encourage us to stick with the things that helped our community come together.

By the late 1960s, Shirley had branched out and developed her own singing group called the Caesar Singers. In 1971 she won her first Grammy Award for the song "Put Your Hand in the Hand of the Man from Galilee." She was the first Black woman to win a Grammy Award in that category since Mahalia Jackson.

A young
Shirley Caesar.

Pastor Caesar would sweep the category for best female gospel singer eleven more times throughout her career.

As her singing career took her all over the globe, she never forsook her calling as a preacher. She founded Mt. Calvary Word of Faith Church in Durham, North Carolina, with her late husband, the Reverend Harold Williams. While she didn't make it to the pulpit every Sunday, when Pastor Caesar was there, she electrified her congregation with her unique blend of songs and sermons that inspired people to run on and see what the end would be.

Broadway came calling for Pastor Caesar in the 1980s and 1990s, when she starred in three plays: *Mama I Want to Sing*, *Mama I Want to Sing, Part II*, and *Born to Sing, Mama I Want to Sing, Part III*.

Vy Higginsen, writer and producer of the *Mama I Want to Sing* trilogy and founder and executive director of the Mama Foundation for the Arts in New York, said, "When I chose Rev. Shirley for the part, it's like she came right out of central casting for a Black woman from the South. She embodied that long history of women in gospel. Every night with her onstage was full of joy, praise, and celebration. There was something in her voice that has a frequency to heal both her and the audience."

Shirley is also no stranger to Hollywood. She has had multiple cameos in movies, including *The Fighting Temptations* and *Why Do Fools Fall in Love?* A brand-new generation caught on to the fiery power of Pastor Caesar in 2016 when her classic song "Hold My Mule" went viral during the Thanksgiving season. Soon after, her songs reentered the gospel charts and went straight to the top. Whether she is making one of her legendary performances at numerous awards ceremonies or preaching the gospel from her home church, Pastor Caesar continues to inspire generations of singers and allows God's people to know that whatever you need from God, all you have to do is believe it and name it!

The United States Postal Service issued the Roberta Martin stamp on July 15, 1998.

Roberta Martin

Born: February 12, 1907
Died: January 18, 1969
Hometown: Helena, Arkansas
Notable Gospel Hits: "God Is Still on the Throne,"
"God Specializes," "He Knows How Much We Can Bear,"
"Try Jesus, He Satisfies"
Awards and Accolades: Known as the Berry Gordy of
gospel music, Roberta Martin wrote and composed
nearly one hundred songs that went on to become
gospel standards. She was honored with a US postage
stamp in 1998.

When Roberta Martin was growing up in Helena, Arkansas, she could not have imagined that her curiosity for learning the piano and making up songs would propel her into the stratosphere of gospel music in its formative years.

One of six children born to William and Anna Winston, Roberta learned to play the piano by the time she was six years old. She learned the fundamentals of playing the gospel scale, finger control, and speed. Like many Black families at the beginning of the twentieth century, Roberta and her family moved north to Chicago during the Great Migration. Once she was settled in Chicago, Roberta had the great fortune of meeting the father of gospel music, Thomas Dorsey. During this time she also began learning how to direct gospel choirs. When Roberta graduated from high school, she attended Northwestern University, and she had high ambitions to become a classical concert pianist.

Roberta's signature sound on the piano and Little Lucy Smith on the Hammond organ helped revolutionize the sound of gospel choirs in Black churches everywhere due to the widespread distribution of her sheet music.

After her marriage to William Martin, Roberta came back to her gospel roots and began her own group, the Roberta Martin Singers. The group's first lineup included Theodore Frye, Robert Anderson, James Lawrence, Norsalus McKissick, Eugene Smith, Romance Watson, and Willie Webb. Many music historians give credit to Roberta for giving gospel music its "beat" and "flavor." Prior to her, hymns were often dry and monotonous. Roberta's signature sound on the piano and Little Lucy Smith on the Hammond organ helped revolutionize the sound of gospel choirs in Black churches everywhere due to the widespread distribution of her sheet music.

After the Roberta Martin Singers gave classic hymns a new flair, these now upbeat and melodious compositions carried the group to Madison Square Garden, Carnegie Hall, and many other venues that rarely invited gospel artists to perform. The Roberta Martin Singers turned out six gold records for the Apollo and Savoy labels, and Roberta composed seventy songs and arranged and published nearly three hundred songs for a wide range of gospel superstars, including James Cleveland and Dorothy Norwood. Roberta was also a savvy businesswoman who was ahead of her time as she established her own gospel music publishing house in Chicago. Before "the Motown Sound," Black America fell in love with the trademark sound of a "Roberta Martin Gospel Song." Roberta was the Berry Gordy of her day and was the creator behind gospel classics like "He Knows How Much We Can Bear," "Try Jesus, He Satisfies," "Only a Look," "I'm Just Waiting on the Lord," and "God Is Still on the Throne."

Roberta died from complications from cancer in 1969, and more than fifty thousand people attended her funeral services. One of her group members, the Reverend Archie Dennis Jr., told the Smithsonian in 1981, "A lot of people have copied or tried to emulate her style of playing, that Roberta Martin sound at the piano and the mixed voices and the style. Mrs. Martin had a certain style of writing music. She didn't write trendy songs. It's just as fresh as it was thirty years ago because it had a message."

21

CROSSOVER QUEENS

Singers Aretha Franklin *(left)* and BeBe Winans perform onstage during the Fiftieth Annual Grammy Awards held at the Staples Center on February 10, 2008, in Los Angeles, California.

Aretha Franklin

Born: March 25, 1942
Died: August 16, 2018
Hometown: Detroit, Michigan
Notable Gospel Hits: "Amazing Grace," "You've Got a Friend," "Climbing Higher Mountains"
Notable Crossover Hits: "Respect," "Say a Little Prayer," "(You Make Me Feel) Like a Natural Woman"
Awards and Accolades: Twenty-six Grammy nominations, eighteen Grammy Awards, Rock and Roll Hall of Fame (1987), Grammy Lifetime Achievement Award (1994), Kennedy Center Honors (1994), Presidential Medal of Freedom (2005), Gospel Music Hall of Fame (2012), Pulitzer Prize (2019)

Aretha Franklin recording at the piano at Columbia Studios in 1962 in New York.

Aretha sang with sisters Erma and Carolyn Franklin and gospel legend Mavis Staples on the 1987 recording *One Lord, One Faith, One Baptism.*

When Aretha Franklin stepped onto the pulpit of the New Temple Missionary Baptist Church in 1972, resplendent in a large green caftan, perfectly coiffed Afro, and turquoise eyeshadow to match, she was a woman in full control of her artistic expression. By the early 1970s, she could have been anywhere in the world. Throughout the 1960s, she dominated the R&B charts with number one hits like "Respect," "Chain of Fools," and "Think." But during two steamy nights in a Los Angeles church, Aretha was back to the core of her gospel roots, recording new renditions of gospel classics, such as "Wholy, Holy," "How I Got Over," and of course "Amazing Grace" that took the audience from tearful reverence to a Holy Ghost frenzy. "It didn't matter how far Aretha went into the world, she was always Reverend C. L. Franklin's daughter and her heart was always in the church," shared George Faison, legendary choreographer and frequent collaborator with the queen of soul throughout her career.

Under the guidance of her mentor, the Reverend James Cleveland, and the soulful singing of the Southern California Community Choir, the recording sessions from those two electric evenings were the foundation of her album *Amazing Grace*, which would go on to become the bestselling gospel album of all time.

"Aretha was a sonic prophet," said Dr. Melanie Hill, acclaimed violinist and author of *Personified Preaching: Black Feminist Sermonic Practice in Literature and Music*. "Her voice reaches generations back into slavery. You can hear the song of the slave woman as she's toiling in the field. At that moment when she is performing at the White House in 2015, you can hear that diasporic, transatlantic sound in Aretha's voice. I believe that is why people loved her all of those years."

Many Black performers of her era were underpaid or even cheated during recording sessions and live performances. So the queen of soul was adamant about being paid in cash and ensuring that every person from her assis-

Aretha Franklin performs during the 2017 Tribeca
Film Festival Opening Gala premiere of *Clive
Davis: The Soundtrack of Our Lives* at Radio City
Music Hall on April 19, 2017, in New York City.

tant to the bandleader was paid accordingly at the end of the night. "There are many things that I will miss about Aretha, but one of the things I will miss the most is that she paid in cash," joked Faison. "The queen was serious about her business, and I appreciated that she ensured that everyone was paid and treated fairly."

Over the next forty years, Aretha would fulfill her title as the queen of soul with more than twenty-six Grammy nominations and eighteen Grammy Awards under her belt. She also received the Presidential Medal of Freedom, the Kennedy Center Honors, and numerous honorary doctorate degrees.

But no matter how far Aretha's amazing voice took her, her gospel foundation was never far from her heart. "Even when she wasn't specifically singing gospel, she was always doing God's work," said Faison. "[Aretha] followed in Mahalia's footsteps and she was always a pure lady."

Aretha never let us forget that it was God's amazing grace that brought her into our hearts and it was his grace that led her home.

Aretha Franklin sings for the crowd at the American Portrait Gala, November 15, 2015, at the National Portrait Gallery in Washington, DC. The honorees of the first Portrait of a Nation Prize at the gala were Aretha Franklin, Hank Aaron, Maya Lin, Carolina Herrera, and Corporal Kyle Carpenter.

Aretha was invited to sing "The Star-Spangled Banner" for former president Barack Obama's first presidential inauguration in 2009, and she was a frequent musical guest of the Obama White House. In 2015, the queen of soul arrived on the stage of the Kennedy Center for one of her last live performances, in a floor-length cream gown and an elegant clutch in her hand. She nodded to the pianist to begin with the opening chords of "Amazing Grace." What came out of her mouth for the next four and a half minutes can only be described as spellbinding. When the camera panned to former president Barack Obama, you could see him wiping away tears.

When the world sent the queen of soul home to be with the Lord in the summer of 2018, it was a nearly ten-hour homegoing service that included legendary singers, preachers, and speakers who celebrated Aretha's nearly sixty years of performance. Aretha never let us forget that it was God's amazing grace that brought her into our hearts, and it was his grace that led her home.

(left to right) Jennifer Hudson, Aretha Franklin, and Janelle Monae pose backstage at BET Honors 2014 at Warner Theatre on February 8, 2014, in Washington, DC.

Aretha Franklin stands
with comedian and actress
Whoopi Goldberg, 1986.

Lauryn Hill and
Aretha Franklin,
January 21, 1998.

First Lady Michelle Obama reaches out to embrace Aretha Franklin as president and CEO of the Martin Luther King Jr. National Memorial Project Foundation Harry Johnson (left), President Barack Obama, Vice President Joe Biden (third right), Biden's wife, Jill, and Interior Secretary Ken Salazar (right) look on after Franklin performed at the dedication of the Martin Luther King Jr. Memorial on October 16, 2011, in Washington, DC.

Singers Aretha Franklin and Al Green are photographed during preparations for the first concert for the Rock and Roll Hall of Fame on September 2, 1995, in Cleveland, Ohio.

Aretha Franklin hugs Smokey Robinson at a rehearsal for the "Aretha Franklin: Duets" concert to benefit the Gay Men's Health Crisis, at the Nederlander Theater in April 1993 in New York City. The concert was taped and broadcast on the Fox Network on May 9, 1993.

Aretha Franklin and LL Cool J at the PS2 Estate during PS2 Estate Day 3 of the Sixth Annual P. Diddy White Party in Bridgehampton, New York.

Alicia Keys and Aretha Franklin attend Keep a Child Alive's Eleventh Annual Black Ball at Hammerstein Ballroom on October 30, 2014, in New York City.

Sister Rosetta Tharpe

Born: March 20, 1915
Died: October 9, 1973
Hometown: Cotton Plant, Arkansas
Notable Gospel Hits: "Down by the Riverside,"
"Up Above My Head," "This Train"
Notable Crossover Hits: "Strange Things Happening
Every Day"
Awards and Accolades: Rock and Roll Hall of Fame
(2017)

Vocalist/guitarist Sister Rosetta Tharpe
(1915–1973) poses for a portrait holding
a guitar in circa 1940 New York City.

Sister Rosetta Tharpe with a group of children from the Tiger Bay area of Cardiff, December 2, 1957.

Before Chuck Berry, Little Richard, and Elvis built the cornerstone for rock and roll, a brassy mocha-colored girl from Cotton Plant, Arkansas, was unwittingly laying its foundation.

Born Rosetta Nubin in a segregated community that devalued girls, young Rosetta grew empowered as she traveled with her talented mother, Katie Bell, singing at various revivals and sanctified church services, first in her town and later throughout the county.

As early as age six, Rosetta possessed a booming voice and played the piano, but it was when she dared to grab the guitar (an instrument typically played by men) that she entered unchartered territory, which would lead her to the Rock and Roll Hall of Fame some forty-five years after her death.

Rosetta enjoyed pushing boundaries and displayed a flair for showmanship throughout her career, which took her from former slave plantations to glitzy venues around the world.

Audiences grew to love the stylish entertainer who slung her electric Gibson guitar across her shoulders and effortlessly plucked the strings, sliding her hand up and down the neck of the wooden instrument to create a gospel chord progression uniquely her own.

"No one had ever seen anything like it!" said Dr. Melanie Hill, noted violinist and author of *Personified Preaching: Black Feminist Sermonic Practice in Literature and Music*. "During these performances with her mother, Rosetta began building a name around the Chicago area and her first performance outside of Chicago was at the Holy Temple Church of God in Christ in Philadelphia."

By the time she was nineteen, Sister Rosetta's innovative style caught the attention of the secular music world. After a short marriage to her first husband, Tommy Tharpe, Rosetta moved to New York City and began performing with Lucky Millinder and His Orchestra. She signed her first record deal in 1938 with Decca Records, a seven-year contract that locked her into singing secular songs and made her lose some of her most dedicated gospel fans. Her Decca recordings unleashed a flurry of mixed church hymns with a blues-style delivery that either converted you into a fan or made you question her faith. "Rosetta's fans were loyal, and they wanted her to sing the gospel," Dr. Hill said. "She would often go back and forth, but ultimately she knew that gospel was really where her heart was."

She traveled widely with Lucky Millinder and His Orchestra and scored hits with songs like "The Lonesome Road" and the distinctly secular "(I Want a) Tall Skinny Papa." In the fall of that year, she also joined the cast of the Cotton Club Revue, which featured Cab Calloway and the Nicholas Brothers dancers. She also played the Paramount Theatre with Count Basie and was one of the first gospel artists to sing at the famed Apollo Theater.

When she was freed from her recording deal with Decca, she was determined to take her career into her own hands. She began collaborating with Marie Knight, and they recorded the gospel hit "Up Above My Head." In 1945,

she recorded what would become her biggest hit, "Strange Things Are Happening Every Day," which was a searing commentary on American life after World War II and the horrendous conditions of the Jim Crow South.

As Rosetta became a marquee name on the chitlin circuit, she also learned how to put on a "show" and keep her name circulating in gossip columns. She was rumored to be bisexual, and after divorcing her first husband, Tommy Tharpe, Rosetta later married Russell Morrison, who was also her manager. But a wedding chapel was small potatoes for the entertainer with big ideas. Unafraid to push the envelope, Rosetta's team made a complete spectacle of her nuptials on July 3, 1951, and staged it inside Griffith baseball stadium in the nation's capital.

More than twenty thousand paying customers attended, dressed in their Sunday best. Some even brought gifts! In a stroke of marketing genius, "the Original Soul Singer," as she became known throughout her life, delivered a rousing concert in her white wedding gown.

Rosetta also made sure the glorious spectacle was recorded and later released as an album. By the early 1950s, Sister Rosetta Tharpe was one paid sister, whose estimated worth was more than two hundred thousand dollars.

In 1964 she starred as one of the headliners for the Blues Festival in London. The wet and windy conditions of the abandoned train station for the festival didn't stop her from belting out her legendary tunes "This Train" and "Down by the Riverside" to an eager audience filled with London teenagers who, hungry for her southern-tinged gospel, clapped and sang along. "She was a trailblazer," Dr. Hill noted. "It wasn't a surprise that her signature sound became the genesis for what would be known as Rock 'N Roll." To her sheer delight, some of the biggest names in music kissed her ring and crowned her "the Godmother of Rock and Roll," which the dimpled singer embraced with great pride. "When people caught on to Rosetta's sound, they would often say, 'She sounds just like Jimi Hendrix, Pete Townshend, and Eric Clapton,'" said noted filmmaker Mick Csaky, who developed a PBS documentary on

Rosetta in 2013. "I would quickly correct them and say, 'No, they sound like HER.' She was the blueprint that they all followed."

As the music scene changed with the times, Sister Rosetta was still in demand because foot-stomping, hand-clapping music never grows old. So whether it was the Apollo Theater, where she was the first gospel singer to take the hallowed stage, or the famed Cotton Club, where she performed with Cab Calloway, Rosetta paved the way for generations of performers. However, after the death of her beloved mother, Katie Bell, and the decline of her health due to diabetes, Rosetta made her last performance singing "Precious Lord" in Copenhagen, Denmark, in 1972. Sister Rosetta Tharpe believed in the power of her own voice, and her testimony of faith unleashed the first spark of Black Girl Magic.

Musicians Brittany Howard, Questlove, and Felicia Collins pay tribute to Sister Rosetta Tharpe during the Thirty-Third Annual Rock and Roll Hall of Fame Induction Ceremony at Public Auditorium on April 14, 2018, in Cleveland, Ohio.

Sister Rosetta Tharpe performing in Copenhagen, Denmark, October 1964.

Mavis Staples

Born: July 10, 1939
Hometown: Chicago, Illinois
Notable Gospel Hits: "Uncloudy Day," "Fix Me Jesus," "Sit Down Servant"
Notable Crossover Hits: "I'll Take You There," "Respect Yourself," "If You're Ready (Come Go with Me)"
Awards and Accolades: Three Grammys, Rock and Roll Hall of Fame (1999), Grammy Lifetime Achievement Award (2005), Kennedy Center Honors (2016)

The Staple Singers circa 1970.

Mavis Staples.

When the Staple Singers took on their first live performance, and Mavis Staples was just thirteen years old, they sang the same song three times for an encore, as the legendary leader of the group, Roebuck "Pops" Staples, taught the burgeoning group only one song from beginning to end.

Five years later, after Mavis graduated from high school—and now with a full roster of songs in tow—the entire family went on the road and took their hand-clapping and foot-stomping music to churches and live venues throughout the country. Mavis couldn't help but be influenced by good music, as her family's South Side Chicago home was constantly filled with singers like Sam Cooke, Curtis Mayfield, Lou Rawls, and gospel legend Mahalia Jackson. The Staple Singers signed their first record deal in 1952 with Vee-Jay Records, and their first recorded single, "Uncloudy Day," was one of the first gospel songs to sell over one million copies.

In an early video recording of the Staple Singers from the 1960s, a young Mavis and her sister Yvonne are clad in choir robes, while her brother Pervis and Pop Staples were sharply dressed in their finest Sunday suits. Mavis's signature voice could be heard on such gospel hits as "Sit Down Servant" and "Fix Me Jesus." Audiences were often surprised to see a young, petite Mavis belting out tunes with a voice that sounded like it belonged to a man or a robust woman twice her size.

After meeting with Dr. Martin Luther King Jr. at the Dexter Avenue Baptist Church in the early 1960s, the Staple Singers began including protest songs in their repertoire. Pops Staples famously said, "If he can preach it, we can sing it." Their frequent performances in the church circuit throughout the South almost landed the legendary quartet in jail. After an altercation with a white gas-station attendant in Memphis in 1964, the Staple Singers were arrested briefly on false robbery and assault charges. The local police captain released them after he recognized who was arrested. Many Black people in the South weren't as

"We went from singing with just Pops on guitar, and then when we went to Stax they put a rhythm section behind us. Everybody would hit the dance floor—including church folks!"

fortunate as the Staple Singers to avoid the atrocities of police brutality and discrimination. This incident further fueled the group to add more protest songs to their performances, such as "Why You Treat Me So Bad?" and "Long Walk to DC." The Staple Singers were invited to perform at larger mainstream venues such as the Newport Folk Festival in 1964.

By the early 1970s, the Staple Singers traded in their church robes and Sunday suits for bell-bottoms, jumpsuits, and sky-high Afros. Their performance at Wattstax in 1972 features Mavis's legendary voice crooning out their biggest hits. One year before this soul-stirring performance, Mavis and the Staple Singers were signed to the legendary Stax Records. In a 2016 interview, Mavis said, "We went from singing with just Pops on guitar, and then when we went to Stax they put a rhythm section behind us. Everybody would hit the dance floor—including church folks!" Their first album with the label yielded the R&B hit "I'll Take You There." Mavis's legendary lead vocals could be heard on subsequent

The Staple Singers performing
circa 1970.

Mavis Staples and Whoopi Goldberg attend the Thirty-Seventh Annual Kennedy Center Honors at the John F. Kennedy Center for the Performing Arts on December 7, 2014, in Washington, DC.

Argentine pianist Martha Argerich, rock band the Eagles, screen and stage actor Al Pacino, gospel and blues singer Mavis Staples, and musician James Taylor are recognized for their achievements in the arts during a star-studded celebration on the Kennedy Center Opera House stage, the Thirty-Ninth Annual Kennedy Center Honors, broadcast on the CBS Television Network. Pictured (left to right): James Taylor, Trevor Noah, Mavis Staples, and President Barack Obama.

Ledisi and Mavis Staples perform during the Fifty-Fourth Annual Grammy Awards Music Preservation Project at Saban Theatre on February 9, 2012, in Beverly Hills, California.

Blues and Rock and Roll Hall of Fame inductee Mavis Staples and the Reverend Jesse Jackson before the game between the Chicago Cubs and the Pittsburgh Pirates at Wrigley Field on July 13, 2019, in Chicago, Illinois.

hits throughout the 1970s, including "Respect Yourself" and "Let's Do It Again." As the Staple Singers welcomed a wider audience and more Top 40 hits throughout the 1970s, they responded to the critics who insisted that they strayed from their gospel roots by proclaiming that the core of their message was always love.

While the Staple Singers' popularity began to slow down during the 1980s, that didn't stop Mavis from continuing to tour as a solo artist and delight audiences all around the world. Her thirteen solo albums include recording with Prince in the 1990s and producing a gospel album in celebration of close family friend and mentor Mahalia Jackson, titled *Spirituals and Gospel: Dedicated to Mahalia Jackson*, and working with legendary blues and bluegrass producer Jeff Tweedy in

the 2000s. She also earned her first of three Grammy Awards in 2005 with her album *One True Vine*.

In 2016, Mavis received the Kennedy Center Honors, and she triumphantly returned as a headliner at the Newport Folk Festival. When Mavis celebrated her eightieth birthday in 2019, there were multiple celebrations to honor her seventy years in the business, with tributes at the Apollo Theater and the Newport Folk Festival and performances by Norah Jones, Jon Baptiste, David Byrne of the Talking Heads, and Ben Harper. She is also a frequent performer at the New Jersey Performing Arts Center, whose director, David Rodriguez, said, "Mavis has a voice that rumbles in my chest for days. Audiences always connect with her because she brings a level of grit, soul, and authenticity to every performance."

CeCe Winans

Born: October 8, 1964
Hometown: Detroit, Michigan
Notable Gospel Hits: "Heaven," "Addictive Love," "Lost Without You," "Alright," "Alabaster Box"
Awards and Accolades: Twelve Grammy Awards and eight Dove Awards

Singer CeCe Winans performs at the Regal Theater in Chicago, Illinois, in December 1989.

CeCe Winans's journey to becoming a gospel diva almost seemed predestined as a member of the legendary Winans family. Her musical roots run deep: her father, David "Pop" Winans, had his own brush with fame, through an opportunity to sing with Sam Cooke in the 1950s, but he turned it down because of his deep conviction to serving Christ. Born as Priscilla Marie Winans in Detroit, Michigan, CeCe was the first daughter in her family, with seven older brothers and two younger sisters. She sang her first solo, "Fill My Cup Lord," at age eight. As her older brothers Ronald, Carvin, Marvin, and Michael were blazing up the gospel charts as the Winans in the early 1980s, CeCe and older brother BeBe were carefully following their blueprint and began their own singing career as part of the Praise the Lord (PTL) singers in 1984. CeCe, who was just nineteen at the time, noted that it was challenging to find her style as a young, petite Black woman in a group of all-white singers. She and BeBe soon found their own light within the group and became well known for their rendition of the

Recording artists Donnie McClurkin and CeCe Winans perform during the Super Bowl Gospel Celebration 2011 at Music Hall at Fair Park on February 4, 2011, in Dallas, Texas.

song "Love Lift Us Up (Where We Belong)." The duo soon scored their first album deal in 1986 and debuted their eponymous record to critical acclaim.

To appreciate the full power that is CeCe Winans, one only has to listen to her duet with her late brother Ron Winans on the powerful gospel song "My Help." When CeCe takes the stage with Ron and his choir, she is elegantly dressed in a sleek all-black suit, and when she opens her mouth, she takes this solemn song from just another choir hymn to powerful anthem that sweeps through the congregation with a powerful praise. Their performance of this song got so good to CeCe and Ron that they blessed the congregation with three reprises of the chorus before they brought the song to a close.

While CeCe is a self-proclaimed introvert and homebody, all those tendencies seem to magically disappear the moment she opens her mouth and allows her fans to experience the unique gift that she pours into every song. "To become a successful gospel singer, you have to have the gospel in your heart," she shared in an interview with *Essence* magazine. "Being a gospel singer is more than a talent, more than just a gift. It's having that spirit. Singing was definitely something that God had planned for my life. My steps were ordered."

By the time BeBe and CeCe's second album, *Heaven*, hit the airwaves in 1988, CeCe shed the conservative looks from her days with PTL and began emerging confidently as a woman with a voice that carried such songs as "Celebrate New Life," "Trust Him," and her searing solo "For Always." This smash album also featured a guest appearance by the late Whitney Houston on the song "Hold Up the Light." CeCe and Houston began a lifelong friendship during this recording, which included CeCe serving as a bridesmaid in Houston's 1992 wedding and becoming the godmother to her daughter, Bobbi Kristina.

When BeBe and CeCe followed up *Heaven* with an even bigger album, *Addictive Love*, in 1990, they were among the first gospel artists to have a music video that was in heavy rotation on BET, VH1, and MTV. While there was backlash from more conservative Christian audiences, CeCe and BeBe charted a path for contemporary gospel artists to confidently and boldly share the Gospel beyond the confines of the church walls.

By the fall of 1995, CeCe decided to branch out and create her first solo album, *Alone in His Presence*. There were many critics around her at the time who were asking, "Why would CeCe break up such a good formula with BeBe?" "Could she carry an entire album on her own?" "Would her audience be willing to buy her music without BeBe?"

None of those questions had time to fester: *Alone in His Presence* brilliantly showcased CeCe's signature alto range and silenced her critics with beautiful songs such as "Every Time," "Blessed Assurance," and a duet with her mother, Deborah Winans, on the cherished gospel hymn "Great Is Thy Faithfulness." Over the next two decades, CeCe released seven solo albums, including a triumphant comeback album with BeBe in 2008 titled *Still*. In 2017, CeCe became one of the first gospel artists to sing with the Nashville Symphony Orchestra, and in 2020, she released her first live-worship album.

Outside her singing talents, CeCe and her husband, Alvin Love, are the pastors of Nashville Life Christian Church, where she is affectionately known as Pastor CeCe. CeCe and Alvin have been married for nearly forty years and have two children, Alvin III and Ashley, and she recently became a grandmother in late 2020.

Whether she's belting out God's goodness with her big brother BeBe or ministering to an audience alone with her rich, warm, melodious voice, CeCe Winans is a gospel legend who heals the soul and inspires every person who hears her voice.

Mary Mary

Group Members and Birth Dates:
Erica Campbell, April 29, 1972
Trecina Evette "Tina" Campbell, May 1, 1974
Hometown: Inglewood, California
Notable Gospel Hits: "Shackles," "Yesterday,"
"The God in Me," "Walking"
Awards and Accolades: Four Grammy Awards

Erica and Tina Campbell.

During the 2007 Stellar Awards, Mary Mary was riding high on the wave of a record ten Stellar nominations and seven wins for their third album, *Mary Mary*. When the duo hit the stage, Erica Atkins shining in a form-fitting, gold, floor-length gown and Tina Atkins matching her sister's swagger in a platinum-silver gown, the packed auditorium was primed to hear the award-winning sisters sing their number one hit, "Yesterday." As Tina squalled the final line, "I decided that I ca-riiied my last tear . . . ," Erica belted out the final word of this soulful ballad in her rich alto, "Yesterdaaaay." By the time Erica dropped the mic from her mouth, the entire audience was on their feet and eager to hear the sisters *sang* just a little while longer. For the next few minutes, the sisters and their equally talented background singers traded soulful riffs and brought the crowd to a soul-filled frenzy.

Long before Mary Mary redefined the landscape of modern gospel music, Erica and Tina were simply the two oldest sisters of the nine siblings who enjoyed singing at their home church in Inglewood, California. Their father, Eddie Atkins, was a preacher, and their mother, Thomasina, played piano and directed the church choir. What the Atkins family lacked in financial resources, they made up in talent, with gospel music becoming the creative engine of the household. While Erica and Tina were content with solos on Sunday and singing background for several gospel groups in Southern California, their talent would soon come to light by way of rising producer Warryn Campbell. Campbell, who became Erica's husband in 2001, had already made a name for himself on several hip-hop and R&B hits in the late 1990s and was now putting his legendary beats behind these sisters in a way that would take the music world by storm. The sisters decided to call themselves Mary Mary after the two prominent Marys in the Bible, Mary, the mother of Jesus, and Mary Magdalene.

When Mary Mary officially burst onto the scene in the spring of 2000 with their electric first single, "Shackles (Praise You)," listeners couldn't immediately tell if the sisters were singing gospel or R&B. Similar to BeBe and CeCe Winans

Erica Campbell performs during Detroit
River Days 2014 at the Detroit Riverfront
on June 22, 2014, in Detroit, Michigan.

Tina Campbell performs during Detroit River Days 2014 at the Detroit Riverfront on June 22, 2014, in Detroit, Michigan.

and Kirk Franklin in the 1990s, Mary Mary's first single quickly rose from the gospel charts and hit R&B radio in record speed. While there was some controversy about the sisters crossing over to a more mainstream audience, one could hear that the sisters hadn't strayed far from their gospel roots on songs such as "Can't Give Up Now" and their funky cover of the classic Negro spiritual "Wade in the Water."

For the next decade, the sisters continued redefining the genre with three gold gospel albums, numerous awards, and another platinum hit, "The God in Me," with Kierra Sheard and Kanye West. Outside their singing careers, the sisters have also made a name for themselves with their hit reality show *Mary Mary* on WE tv. Erica and Tina became the first gospel artists to have a reality show on cable television. They also served as judges on the gospel singing competition *Sunday Best*. While some of their core fans criticized the sisters for showing the world their lives behind the scenes of their reality show as mothers, wives, and sometimes as dueling sisters who fought each other hard to bring their message to the world, they also gained a new legion of fans who appreciated the sisters' vulnerability

Erica Campbell and Tina Campbell of Mary Mary pose in the press room at the Fifty-First Annual Grammy Awards held at the Staples Center on February 8, 2009, in Los Angeles, California.

and their openness about being flawed, imperfect, yet forgiven Christian women. The sisters were also vulnerable about their marriages to the respective husbands, Warryn Campbell and Teddy Campbell, who coincidentally share the same last name but are not related, and being mothers to their children. Erica and Warryn are the parents of three children; Teddy and Tina share five children.

Mary Mary won a Grammy for their album *Something Big* in 2011, and since then both singers have continued blessing the world with their respective solo projects. Tina released her first solo album, *It's Still Personal*, and an accompanying book in 2017, and Erica expanded her talents to the radio and is now host of the show *Get Up with Erica* and First Lady of the California Worship Center. Erica also released her solo album *Help*, which featured the chart-topping single "I Need Just a Little More Jesus." With their fiery energy and swagalicious delivery to sing the good news of the Gospel, the world most likely hasn't heard the last from Mary Mary, and their fans eagerly await more from this duo, who have redefined what it means to be saved, cool, and unapologetically on fire for Christ.

Erica Atkins-Campbell and Tina Atkins of Mary Mary perform at Prospect Park Bandshell on June 21, 2012, in the Brooklyn borough of New York City.

Mary Mary perform during the 2011 Soul Train Awards at the Fox Theatre on November 17, 2011, in Atlanta, Georgia.

5

AND STILL SHE SHOUTS

Honoree Tamela Mann accepts the James Cleveland Lifetime Achievement Award during the Thirty-Third Annual Stellar Gospel Music Awards at the Orleans Arena on March 24, 2018, in Las Vegas, Nevada.

Tamela Mann

Born: June 9, 1966

Hometown: Limestone County, Texas

Notable Gospel Hits: "Take Me to the King," "Change Me," "God Provides," "We Need a Touch from You"

Awards and Accolades: One Grammy Award, one Billboard Award, one BET Award, two NAACP Image Awards, and two GMA Awards

Singer Tamela Mann at the Premiere Ceremony during the Fifty-Ninth Grammy Awards at Microsoft Theater on February 12, 2017, in Los Angeles, California.

Tamela Mann performs during the Thirty-Second Annual Stellar Gospel Music Awards at the Orleans Arena on March 25, 2017, in Las Vegas, Nevada.

By June 2020, America was weary, frightened, and exhausted from the ongoing horrors of the coronavirus pandemic. Black America, in particular, was traumatized by the brutal killing of yet another unarmed Black man, George Floyd, at the hands of the Minneapolis Police Department. On the first Sunday afternoon of that month, there was a sliver of hope when gospel giants Fred Hammond and Kirk Franklin went head-to-head in a battle of their greatest hits on the Instagram Live series *Verzuz*. Midway through the set, Franklin stepped behind a keyboard and started playing a familiar melody. And then suddenly there she was—Tamela Mann showed up on the other side of our screens and began singing "Truth is I'm tired / Options are few / I'm trying to pray / But where are you?" In a moment where everything in the world felt upside down, for three minutes and thirty seconds, Tamela took us to the throne of grace with a stripped-down version of her megahit "Take Me to the King," with a beauty and force that brought some much-needed peace to our souls.

Tamela Mann has been taking us to the king for quite some time. Born and raised in Limestone County, Texas, the youngest of fourteen children, Tamela began singing with the choir in the Church of God in Christ. She grew up in a very strict Pentecostal household, but she was able to listen to Andraé Crouch, the Caravans, and the Hawkins Family, who would eventually influence her sound. By the time she was twelve years old, she already had a number of solos under her belt. Tamela was also inspired by the R&B singer Stacy Lattisaw.

Just as Tamela's confidence began to blossom in high school, so did her love life. She met her future husband, David Mann, in 1978, and this union connected her not only with her soul mate but also to the man who would become her partner in sparking her dream and purpose to minister to the world through song.

Soon after their union, Tamela and David were recruited to join a new gospel group with their good friend Kirk Franklin, called the Family. Tamela's soaring soprano can be heard on

Tamela Mann performs during "Mann's World Concert and Comedy Show" at James L. Knight Center on September 1, 2017, in Miami, Florida.

David and Tamela Mann perform onstage at the David and Tamela "Against the World" Family Tour on October 13, 2018, in Los Angeles, California.

several of the Family's biggest hits, including "Now Behold the Lamb" and "Lean on Me."

After five albums with the Family, Tamela and David formed their own label, Tillymann Music Group, and Tamela released her first solo album, *Gotta Keep Movin'*, in 2005. Tamela's huge breakthrough came with 2012's *Better Days*, which shattered gospel music industry records with the Franklin-penned single "Take Me to the King." The single debuted at number one on the gospel music charts and stayed there for an astonishing nineteen weeks.

As if her singing talents weren't enough, Tamela also branched out as an actress and is affectionately known as the delightful and devout Cora Brown in several plays, movies, and television series by Tyler Perry, including *Diary of a Mad Black Woman*, *Madea Goes to Jail*, *Madea's Big Happy Family*, and *Tyler Perry's Meet the Browns*. Tamela and David often share the screen together, as he plays the over-the-top and hilarious Deacon Brown. The duo has also ventured into reality TV with their show *It's a Mann's World* and produced a cooking show, *Hanging with the Manns*. This mother of five and grandmother of eight has also become a beacon of hope for many plus-size women, as she courageously shared her health and weight loss journey and developed and designed an athleisure line catered for plus-size women.

With her vision clear, Tamela has a mission to continue ministering the gospel for as long as she can. "There's still love and hope and compassion in the world," she says. "There is always an opportunity for me to show His love and His grace. My heart's desire is to get His message out, to let people know that He still lives."

Tamela Mann performs during the 2013 BET Awards at Nokia Plaza LA Live on June 30, 2013, in Los Angeles, California.

Dottie Peoples

Born: August 12, 1950

Hometown: Dayton, Ohio

Notable Gospel Hits: "On Time God," "Surely God Is Able," "Is It Worth It All?"

Awards and Accolades: Five Stellar Awards (1995, 2010), James Cleveland Lifetime Achievement Award (1997)

Gospel singer Dottie Peoples performs during the opening night of Theo London's inspirational staged play *Loving Him Is Killing Me*, at James L. Knight Center on May 13, 2011, in Miami, Florida.

Dottie Peoples taping BET's *Bobby Jones Gospel Show*, Washington, DC.

In the summer of 1994, a song with a simple one-chorus melody and a funky guitar line was slowly creeping its way from local gospel radio station WOAK in Atlanta and soon began popping up on gospel playlists throughout the country. By the fall of that year, you couldn't go anywhere without hearing Dottie Peoples's "On Time God" everywhere from nail and hair salons on Saturday afternoons to the choir lofts on Sunday morning. By the time of the 1995 Stellar Awards, Peoples was the belle of the ball, and she triumphantly took home four Stellar Awards for a song that encouraged millions of believers around the world.

While "On Time God" was the first time that many people heard Dottie's powerful voice and saw her immaculate style that included beautiful updos and finely tailored suits, she was far from an overnight success. The oldest of ten children, born in Dayton, Ohio, Dottie began developing her rich alto voice during summers with her beloved grandmother, Big Mama, in Birmingham, Alabama. Big Mama would fill Dorothy's summers with church all

> "So many folks come up to me, some of them crying, some of them just hugging me, some of them so excited. Just to know that you've touched their lives and blessed them like that— it's a feeling that you never ever get over."

day on Sunday and the music of Mahalia Jackson and the Caravans. Dottie fell in love with Mahalia's voice and began imitating her style as she joined choirs at her local church and high school. When she sang her first solo at nine years old, Dottie was astounded by the audience's reaction. "I remember singing and running out of the church," she said. "I got scared because everybody was shouting." Dottie credits Shirley Caesar as one of her biggest inspirations and mentors, and Dottie was often called "Little Shirley" as she was developing her sound as a teenager.

Dottie became a local sensation in Dayton and soon caught the ear of one of the original Caravans, Dorothy Norwood. Norwood invited Dottie to join her on a tour with the Rolling Stones. Dottie's mother initially objected, but Norwood promised to take good care of Dottie while they were on the road. Dottie's experience with Norwood became a hands-on education in vocal performance and gospel delivery. Dottie also met many of her idols, including Stevie Wonder and the Reverend Shirley Caesar.

After touring with Norwood throughout the 1970s, Peoples developed a following as a jazz vocalist for nearly five years. When she moved to Atlanta in 1979, she joined the Salem Baptist Church and was invited to sing her first solo with the choir. She sang a song called "If You Move Yourself." That solo became a pivotal moment for Dottie, and she decided to devote her life to singing gospel music. "It changed my whole life because I stood there and realized that I was blessing people," she shared. "Burdens were being lifted. I knew I didn't want to sing jazz anymore. I just want to sing for the Lord. I got back to my roots and I've been singing gospel ever since."

In 1980, Dottie became the general manager of Church Door Records and released her first two albums on the label, *Surely God Is Able* and *Is It Worth It All?* Dottie's career soon rocketed from local listeners in Atlanta to national acclaim with the little song that could, "On Time God." There were some murmurs in the gospel industry about whether the song could compete with the success of gospel heavy hitters at the time such as Fred Hammond and CeCe Winans, and big choirs like Hezekiah Walker and the Love Fellowship Crusade Choir. But Dottie proved them all wrong with a song that catapulted her to stages all over the globe, gaining national endorsements, performing the national anthem at the Centennial Olympics and Atlanta Hawks basketball games, becoming the first gospel singer to debut with the Atlanta Symphony Orchestra, and hosting and producing her own radio show.

Dottie continues to be a staple on the gospel music circuit, with annual performances at the Essence Music Festival and churches throughout the country. Her passion to continue reaching people for Christ keeps this tireless singer going. "What makes me love what I do more than anything is people," she says. "So many folks come up to me, some of them crying, some of them just hugging me, some of them so excited. Just to know that you've touched their lives and blessed them like that—it's a feeling that you never ever get over."

Tramaine Hawkins

Born: October 11, 1951

Hometown: San Francisco, California

Notable Gospel Hits: "Changed," "What Shall I Do?," "The Potter's House," "Going Up Yonder"

Awards and Accolades: James Cleveland Lifetime Gospel Award, three Grammy Awards

American gospel singer
Tramaine Hawkins
circa 1970.

Whether she is belting out a song from a pew or guiding the next generation of gospel singers, Tramaine's legendary voice is always ready to proclaim the good news of Jesus Christ.

Lady Tramaine Hawkins sings onstage during Michael Clarke Duncan's memorial service at Forest Lawn Cemetery on September 10, 2012, in Los Angeles, California.

The world was first introduced to the holy instrument that is Tramaine Hawkins's voice on the groundbreaking gospel album *Love Alive*. Born in San Francisco and raised in Oakland, California, Tramaine began singing at the age of four at the Ephesians Church of God in Christ in Berkeley, which was pastored by her grandfather Bishop E. E. Cleveland. The night she was born, her mother, Lois, sang on the church's broadcast and then was rushed to the hospital to give birth to a little girl who would eventually blossom into one of the most recognizable voices in modern gospel music. She spent summer vacations with her aunt, evangelist Ernestine Cleveland Reems, performing at churches and revival meetings around the country. Hawkins recorded her first single at age ten, singing "He's All Right" with the Heavenly Tones for the Music City label. Tramaine was just fifteen years old when the group recorded their first album in 1966, and the group was soon recruited by Sly and the Family Stone for background vocals on their first album. When Tramaine declined to sing with Sly Stone, that

The Edwin Hawkins Singers,
US vocal group, circa 1969.

opened the door for her to begin singing with gospel legend Andraé Crouch. She sang lead on the group's Grammy-nominated Liberty single "Christian People."

While the call of R&B fame was tempting, Tramaine stayed true to her gospel roots and soon connected with the Edwin Hawkins Singers. She was featured on the hit single "Oh Happy Day," and she began collaborating with her former husband and frequent collaborator, Walter Hawkins, on the *Love Alive* albums. Tramaine's signature soprano solos were featured on the songs "Changed," "Holy One," and "Goin' Up Yonder." Many of these songs, in particular "Goin' Up Yonder," have become standards in today's modern worship services. Tramaine's solos were often so powerful and Holy Ghost filled that they featured epic reprises that would often go on for minutes at a time.

By 1979, Tramaine branched out into what would become a dynamic four-decade solo career. Her first single, "Look at Me," served as a declaration of her place in the pantheon of dynamic gospel sopranos and her devotion to

God and her ministry. By the mid-1980s, Tramaine shocked the gospel music industry when she divorced Walter Hawkins and left the legendary Hawkins family, and her music began climbing up the dance charts. In 1986, her hit "Fall Down" was in heavy rotation at clubs like Studio 54. She even performed at the legendary venue to an audience of nearly four thousand club goers. Soon her loyal fans declared that she was switching to the "Devil's Music." The cut was considered too secular by many and caused a rift in the gospel community.

Her live album in 1990 became a gold-selling gospel classic and featured a soul-filled duet with Walter Hawkins, "The Potter's House." While Tramaine and Walter had long since divorced by the time the single rose up the gospel charts, the chemistry between their voices was undeniable, and the song's heartfelt message of God's ability to mend even the most brokenhearted resonated with both gospel and secular audiences alike. This recording became a fan favorite and earned Tramaine the Grammy Award for Best Traditional Soul Gospel Album in 1991.

Tramaine has continued her illustrious career well into the new millennium with guest appearances on albums with Pastor Donnie McClurkin and Bishop Hezekiah Walker. You can also hear Tramaine's legacy and influence on singers such as Yolanda Adams and Tina Campbell of Mary Mary. Tramaine was a featured soloist at the funerals of Sammy Davis Jr. and Rosa Parks, and Tramaine's son, Jamie, has carried on her legacy as a producer, musician, and songwriter on several of her albums and has branched out to his own solo projects.

Fifty years after her first solo, you could still hear the power of her voice on the evening of Pastor Donnie McClurkin's sixtieth birthday at the Perfecting Faith Church in Freeport, New York, in the fall of 2019. There was an epic mic toss through the audience, featuring the Walter Hawkins classic "Changed." The mic was passed between gospel legends Marvin Winans, Erica Campbell from Mary Mary, and CeCe Winans. But then the mic stopped with the original soloist for this epic gospel anthem, Tramaine Hawkins. She was elegantly dressed in a black suit with multicolored sequins, and she clearly didn't want to draw too much attention to herself, as she began singing while she was still seated. But about forty-five seconds into her solo, she rose from her pew and released the anointing from that legendary soprano voice as only Tramaine Hawkins could do.

Whether she is belting out a song from a pew or guiding the next generation of gospel singers, Tramaine's legendary voice is always ready to proclaim the good news of Jesus Christ.

Kim Burrell

Born: August 26, 1972
Hometown: Houston, Texas
Notable Gospel Hits: "Holy Ghost," "Calvary," "Here I Am," "Someone to Watch Over Me," "Everlasting Life"
Awards and Accolades: Three Stellar Awards (one in 2000, two in 2012), one Dove Award

Kim Burrell is the definition of your favorite singer's singer. Her signature jazzy vocals and out-of-this-world riffs, scats, and runs during her performances leave her audience mesmerized and the most dedicated music fans in disbelief over the sounds that Kim put into their ears.

While gospel music fans had been relishing Kim's mind-blowing vocal ability for years, the world at large came to know her during a very special performance for her friend, the late legendary Whitney Houston. During the 2010 BET Honors, Kim dedicated a soulful version of Houston's cover of "I Believe in You and Me" during this televised ceremony. This was the first time that many of her gospel fans would hear her sing in a secular venue. Kim also showed up that night with a newly svelte figure that she beautifully highlighted with a long, elegant one-shoulder black gown. As she made her way through the performance, a delighted Whitney Houston jumped up from her seat and ran to the front of the stage and yelled at Kim to keep on singing. It didn't matter that this was a formal event; Houston clearly responded to Kim's voice just like it was Sunday morning service. That night Kim's star rose from the church pew and onto the world's stage.

The daughter of a pastor and an evangelist, Kim began the journey to superstardom in her native Houston, Texas. Legend has it that she sang her first solo at just one year old. As a young adult, Kim refined her vocal chops with Rev. James Cleveland's Gospel Music Workshop Choir, Trinity Temple Full Gospel Mass Choir of Dallas, and the Inspirational Sounds Mass Choir of Houston. Kim released her first solo album, *Try Me Again*, in 1995, and the buzz around her debut was so hot that she was signed to Tommy Boy Gospel, which released her sophomore album, *Everlasting Life*, in 1999 and her dynamic live album in 2001. *Everlasting Life* rose to number ten on the Billboard Gospel Music chart, and her live album was nominated for a Grammy Award for Best Contemporary Soul Gospel Album.

Throughout the early 2000s, Kim was in high demand both inside and outside the gospel industry. She was featured on collaborations with Hezekiah Walker, Yolanda Adams, Kirk Franklin, Shirley Caesar, Stevie Wonder, R. Kelly, Missy Elliot, Harry Connick Jr., and George Clinton. She released the albums *No Ways Tired* in 2008 and *The Love Album* in 2011. One of her biggest hits was the title track from the movie *Hidden Figures*, "I See a Victory" with legendary R&B producer Pharrell Williams.

Kim Burrell performs during the 2010 BET Honors at the Warner Theatre on January 16, 2010, in Washington, DC.

Yolanda Adams

Born: August 27, 1961
Hometown: Houston, Texas
Notable Gospel Hits: "Open My Heart," "I've Got the Victory," "Through the Storm," "Just a Prayer Away," "The Battle Is Not Yours (It's the Lord's)"
Awards and Accolades: Five Grammy Awards, four Dove Awards, sixteen Stellar Awards, five BET Awards, one American Music Award, Gospel Music Hall of Fame, and Presidential Lifetime Achievement Award (2016)

Singer/songwriter Yolanda Adams performs during the Fifty-Fifth Annual Grammy Awards Music Preservation Project "Play It Forward" at the Saban Theatre on February 7, 2013, in Los Angeles, California.

Yolanda Adams performing in "A Grammy Salute to the Sounds of Change."

Yolanda Adams always has the perfect ability to deliver the voice of God just when we need it most. Just a few short weeks after the untimely death of pop icon Whitney Houston in 2012, Adams took the stage at the NAACP Image Awards to honor her with a song that Houston made famous from *The Preacher's Wife* soundtrack, "I Love the Lord." When Adams stepped to the mic in all her six-foot-one-inch glory, all eyes were glued to her statuesque frame as she began the song with a controlled reverence and sweetness in her signature soprano. That sweetness soon became a fiery blaze, as Adams and the twenty-five-member choir behind her swelled into the chorus, "I'll hasten to his throne!," with a ferocity that beautifully honored Houston's legacy and ensured listeners in that auditorium and beyond those walls that God's love is truly the balm to soothe and save our souls.

Adams began developing her signature voice in her hometown church in Houston, Texas. The oldest of her six siblings, Yolanda started

fine-tuning her voice by listening to singers she loved in the church. "Growing up in the church was paramount for me. That's where I got the vocal training, I was able to be near folks with powerful voices and folks with melodic voices," she said. "It is the greatest way to start your life—because you have a faith base—and to also start your vocal training. There is no other place more magnificent when it comes to vocal training than the church."

While you can hear the deep roots of gospel music in Yolanda's voice, she also credits her wide exposure to a variety of music in her home with helping her further develop her sound. "I've always listened to music outside of gospel. I grew up listening to a plethora of genres in my house," Yolanda said. "My mom and dad played everything from blues to bluegrass to box [music]. We heard everything. There's so many genres that I admire, especially jazz and symphony, pop and rock. I really grew up on all those things. Thank God I was not one of those kids who had to sneak out to listen to that music. It was right there in my house."

Yolanda first hit the gospel airwaves in 1982 as the lead soloist on the Southern Inspirational Choir's hit "My Liberty." As the song began to climb up the charts, Yolanda was still working as an elementary school teacher. Shortly thereafter, she was discovered by music legend and tastemaker Thomas Whitfield. Under Whitfield's tutelage, Yolanda began branching out with guest appearances on albums with the legendary Edwin Hawkins and gospel producer and pianist Ben Tankard.

She soon found her way to her own spotlight with her debut album *Just as I Am* in 1987. The song and album that truly cracked open Yolanda's career on gospel radio was "Riding Through the Storm." While Yolanda was certainly a household name among her gospel fan base, her voice picked up a new audience with the emergence of her 1999 album *Mountain High . . . Valley Low*. Produced by R&B hit makers Jimmy Jam and Terry Lewis, this album ushered in a new chapter in Yolanda's career with the single "Open My Heart" that propelled her to stardom and the top of the gospel, R&B, and adult contemporary

Singers Israel Houghton (*left*) and Yolanda Adams perform onstage during the Thirtieth Annual Stellar Gospel Music Awards at the Orleans Arena on March 28, 2015, in Las Vegas, Nevada.

Yolanda Adams performs during the New Orleans Jazz and Heritage Festival, April 30, 2006, in New Orleans, Louisiana.

charts. *Mountain High . . . Valley Low* sold more than two million copies and garnered her a Grammy Award. "My goal every time I go into the studio is to take out of my heart and put it on whatever tape and give it to people who need it," Yolanda said. "If people are dealing with wondering about the economy, let's talk about that. If they're thinking about the love of their life, let's do a song about that. If they're thinking about loss, let's talk about that. Let's sing what the heart of the people need right now. I've never gone into the studio and said let's do a song that will go on mainstream radio or let's do a song that will go to the top of the gospel charts. That has never been my thinking. My thinking process is always, 'Who needs this right now?'"

After this crossover success, Yolanda became a staple on many award shows, including the BET Awards, the NAACP Image Awards, and the Soul Train Awards. And the hits just kept on coming with the 2005 release of her album *Day by Day*, which included the megahit "Victory" that opened the doors for Yolanda to

Yolanda Adams, winner for Best Gospel Artist during the Second Annual BET Awards Show, at the Kodak Theater in Hollywood, California.

Adams poses backstage with her award for Favorite Contemporary Inspirational Artist at the Twenty-Ninth Annual American Music Awards in Los Angeles, California, on January 9, 2002.

perform in mainstream venues like *The Today Show* and *The Tonight Show* with Jimmy Fallon. She also served as a judge on the gospel singing contest *Sunday Best* on BET.

As the reigning queen of gospel music, Yolanda has recorded nearly twenty albums, with sales in excess of 4.5 million copies. This dynamic songstress has kept her vibrant career going because of her strong belief in evolving the sound and message of gospel music. "I think

music in general has evolved—the sound has evolved, the electronics have evolved, technology has evolved," she shares. "So, we're just like everyone else and have evolved with the times. When you have Mahalia Jackson singing at the Montreux Jazz Festival or the Newport Jazz Festival back then, you know that people saw gospel as a necessary genre. Everything evolves, and hopefully we are the leaders in those changing times and remain the sound people can relate to."

Singer Yolanda Adams performs onstage at the
Music Preservation Project "Play It Forward" on
February 7, 2013, in Los Angeles, California.

(left to right) Taylor Ayanna Crawford, singer Yolanda Adams, and guest attend the 2014 BET Awards at Nokia Theatre LA Live on June 29, 2014, in Los Angeles, California.

Susan L. Taylor and Yolanda Adams attend an intimate celebration of Taylor's thirty-seven years at *Essence* magazine, at a private residence on December 2, 2008, in New York City.

Yolanda Adams rehearsing for the Thirty-Seventh Annual
A Capitol Fourth, a celebration for Independence Day,
on the West Lawn of the US Capitol, on July 3, 2017.

Yolanda Adams performing during the inaugural "Grammy Jam Fest" at the Wiltern Theatre, December 11, 2004, in Los Angeles, California. The event celebrated the music of Earth, Wind and Fire and raised funds for various arts charities.

Cissy Houston.

Acknowledgments

First and foremost, I want to thank my editor and dear friend Patrik Henry Bass of Amistad for dreaming up this book. When it comes to gospel music, we are kindred spirits. Patrik and I were both raised in holiness churches in New York City, and together we have met and collaborated with many of the gospel artists featured in this historical book through the Essence Music Festival. Thank you, Patrik, for being not just a brilliant editor but also a cherished friend.

I'm also indebted to writer and researcher Leah Lakins, who dived into this project with great enthusiasm! Gospel, of course, means good news, and Leah and I joyfully worked together, eager to share the good news about these amazing women, some of whom died without receiving their just due. Thank you, Leah, for putting your whole soul into *Isn't Her Grace Amazing!*

I'd also like to express my gratitude to my literary agent, Lois de la Haba, a legend in her own right. Lois, thanks for being my best advocate!

Emanuel Robinson proved to be an integral part of this journey. My childhood friend has been at my side as we fanned out over the elegant Yolanda Adams backstage at many Essence Festivals over the years. Together we also got to know the sassy Kim Burrell and we were relieved to know that so many of these stars were down-to-earth. Meeting Tina and Erica Campbell of Mary Mary backstage in New Orleans was a special treat, and, Emanuel, together we have memories to last a lifetime! Thanks for being part of this amazing journey!

It's never easy to pin down a celebrity long enough to talk about themselves. They're always shuttling between airports and juggling demanding schedules. But

Dionne Warwick dropped everything to talk to me about her family's gospel legacy! It was a jaw-dropping moment to see this Grammy-winning music legend up close as she proudly shared precious memories. Ms. Warwick, I can't thank you enough for opening your heart. I only pray that we did the Drinkard Singers justice. My sincere gratitude also goes out to Mr. Angelo Ellerbee of Double XXposure Media Relations Inc.

It was also a thrill to get pearls of wisdom from the great Vy Higginsen, the keeper of the flame of gospel music through her Mama Foundation for the Arts based out of Harlem! Higginsen wears many hats and cast the great Shirley Caesar in her legendary gospel production *Mama, I Want to Sing*. Vy, what an honor to know you and call you a dear friend!

George Faison is another legend I'm proud to call a friend. The Tony Award–winning choreographer of *The Wiz* was a very close friend of Aretha Franklin and several other singers featured in this book, and he was more than happy to share his recollections. Georgie, I hope you know how much I absolutely adore you!

I also want to give a fist bump to Mr. Apollo, Billy Mitchell! The official historian of the Apollo Theater in Harlem has seen it all, from Mahalia Jackson to Yolanda Adams. You're an eyewitness to Black music history and I'm so grateful that you are part of this project, my friend.

I also want to acknowledge Dr. Melanie Hill, who has a special affection for the women featured on these pages and has devoted her scholarly works to amplifying their messages. Special thanks also to Rev. Barbara Riley, gospel historian Tim Dillinger, and Larry Clark, the son of the founder of the Clark Sisters' Denise

Clark. Special thanks also goes out to Micah Coleman, proud grandson of Thelma Davis-Blessingame of the Davis Sisters.

A quick bear hug to my circle of trust, who are always in my corner: Geralyn Lucas, Betsy Berg, Ian Kleinert, Debbie Modeste, Dr. Audrey Baker, Dr. Gerry Baker, Ruschell Boone, Helen Swenson, Sandy, Philip & Gabrielle Hawkins, Dorissa White, Lloyd Williams, Irene Gandy, Rachel Noerdlinger, Annais Morales, Camille Joseph, Rodney Capel, Frank Dilella, Helen Shelton, Paula Edme, Jackie Pinkhard Arrington, Dr. Marcella Maxwell, Lorna Rainey, Tara Riley Patrick, Lewis Dodley, Dominique Sharpton, Ashley Sharpton, Cheryl Brody Franklin, Rachel Vassel, Donyshia Boston-Hill, Dr. Hazel Dukes, and Marilyn Crawford.

Proud to be linked in friendship with my sisters of the Greater Queens Chapter of The Links, Inc.

Eternal love to my husband, John Jr., and my son, John III. Started from the bottom, now we here! Thanks for always being there for me through my sleepless nights and working around the clock!

Lastly, my deepest gratitude to my mother, Ruth. She wasn't a singer like my grandma Opal, but she made sure all five of her children were in church every Sunday morning. I love you, Mommy, for your leadership and guidance. You were right there on the church pew with us because you knew the Bible was right when it says: train up a child in the way they should go and they will not depart from it. I've come a long way, but I have not and will not depart from the life lessons I learned in Sunday school. And, of course, my siblings are the wind beneath my wings: Clarence Jr., Crystal, Celestial, and Cleavon.

And finally, you'll recall I dedicated this historic book to my beloved grandmother, Sister Opal Wills (1927–2019). And in the Introduction I explained how she was a powerful gospel singer in her own right, even though she never cut a record. Well, even as a child, I knew Grandma's voice was something special. So I would tape her on my trusty cassette recorder (remember those?) just about everywhere we went. So if you visit my website, cherylwills.com, it will direct you to my YouTube channel, where you can hear Sister Wills sing the gospel classic "This Old Soul of Mine," made famous by gospel singer Marie Knight (1920–2009). By the way, Knight is pictured in this historic book with Sister Rosetta Tharpe on page 136. My grandma is clearly influenced by Knight's rendition, but you will hear how Sister Wills made this song all her own. She was certainly in her element.

During one of our family's musical family reunions in Cleveland, Ohio, in 1983, Sister Wills (née Tyus) is introduced to the stage by her sister Katherine (Polly) Thomas, and she is accompanied on the piano by another talented sister, Laura Lee (née Tyus), a brilliant pianist who gained fame as a gospel recording artist in her own right. On the organ is Grandma's baby sister, Mary Ruth Spearman (née Tyus), another gifted singer and gospel recording artist.

On the drums is my cousin Bilal Whitest and, most importantly, my grandmother's pride and joy backs her up on lead guitar, her only surviving son at the time, Van Wills. Uncle Van (1945–2006) was a brilliant and gifted guitarist who played with the gospel group the Thrashing Wonders (led by Billie Brown) for more than forty years. The audio is not the best, but you can hear Grandma's booming alto voice loud and clear and her testimony before she sings.

You will also hear me on the tambourine, I try not to play because the cassette recorder is in my lap, but at certain points I can't resist. Especially when folks start shouting when Grandma "brings it home" at the end.

Sister Wills electrifies the church, and when the folks start running around the sanctuary, I get so caught up in the moment, I didn't notice that the cassette tape ran out. Give it a listen and you'll see why.

That old grandma of mine was something else!

My grandmother Sister Opal Wills singing in church
with her guitarist son, Van Wills, backing her up.
She really knew how to move the crowd.

Credits

About the Author

Cheryl Wills is an author and Emmy Award–winning television journalist with Spectrum News. A native New Yorker, she has written a series of children's books about her great-great-great-grandfather Sandy Wills, an enslaved Tennessee man who successfully fought for his freedom during the Civil War. A graduate of Syracuse University, Cheryl anchors a nightly primetime newscast based out of New York City on the cable network NY1, and she also hosts the weekly public affairs talk show *In Focus with Cheryl Wills*. The veteran journalist has won numerous awards throughout her career, including a prestigious medal of excellence from the United Nations Correspondents Association, and she was named one of New York's 25 Most Remarkable Women by *City & State* magazine. In 2018, Cheryl was honored with the prestigious Commander's Medal from the US Department of the Army, one of the highest public service decorations for a civilian. She also received an honorary doctorate from New York College of Health Professions in 2005. Cheryl is married and lives in a suburb of New York City with her husband, John, and her son, John III.